The Life You Deserve

A GUIDE TO MAKING THE FINANCIAL CHOICES THAT
CAN BRING CONFIDENCE AND PROSPERITY

Keith Singer, JD CFP®

Copyright © 2021 by Keith Singer.

All rights reserved. No part of this publication may be reproduced, distributed or transmitted in any form or by any means, including photocopying, recording, or other electronic or mechanical methods, without the prior written permission of the publisher, except in the case of brief quotations embodied in critical reviews and certain other noncommercial uses permitted by copyright law. For permission requests, write to the publisher.

   Keith Singer/Singer Wealth
   1515 S Federal Hwy, Suite #302
   Boca Raton, FL 33432
   https://keithsinger.com/

The Life You Deserve/Keith Singer. —1st ed.

ISBN 9798742772149

Singer Wealth is an independent financial services firm helping individuals create retirement strategies using a variety of investment and insurance products to custom suit their needs and objectives.

Investment advisory services offered through Singer Wealth Advisors, a registered investment advisory firm.

Investing involves risk, including the potential loss of principal. No investment strategy can guarantee a profit or protect against loss in periods of declining values. None of the information contained on this website shall constitute an offer to sell or solicit any offer to buy a security or any insurance product.

The purpose of this book is to provide general information on the subjects discussed, it is not intended to be used as the sole basis for financial decisions, nor should it be construed as advice designed to meet the particular needs of an individual's situation. Our firm does not provide tax or legal advice; all individuals are encouraged to seek guidance from qualified professionals regarding their personal situation.

Any references to protection benefits or steady and reliable income streams on this website refer only to fixed insurance products. They do not refer, in any way, to securities or investment advisory products. Annuity guarantees are backed by the financial strength and claims-paying ability of the issuing insurance company. Annuities are insurance products that may be subject to fees, surrender charges and holding periods which vary by insurance company. Annuities are not FDIC insured.

I am dedicating this book…
To my clients, whose trust I don't take for granted. I am grateful for the intimate relationships that we have developed, and I am honored that you allowed me to become your trusted advisor and that you have placed your confidence in me to serve as your guide through life's financial trials and tribulations.

To my wife Mishelle, who has given me her unwavering support and love.

To my children Jake, Aidan, Eli, and Sara, who continue to inspire me to be the best person I can be. I am proud that both Jake and Aidan obtained their securities licenses while still in their teens and I am excited to watch the future accomplishments of my children.

To my parents, who taught me the value of a dollar and instilled in me my work ethic.

To the dedicated staff and advisors of Singer Wealth Advisors who have embraced our company's culture and passion for delivering the very best customized advice and service to our clients.

To the other advisors who have generously shared ideas and best practices and to The Strategic Coach and Advisors Excel, who have provided me with invaluable advice and assistance.

Table of Contents

INTRODUCTION:
THE LIFE YOU DESERVE 1

CHAPTER ONE:
THE LAW OF GIVING 3

CHAPTER TWO:
"I DON'T NEED ANYONE'S HELP" 7

CHAPTER THREE:
FROM SOLVING PROBLEMS TO PREVENTING THEM 11

CHAPTER FOUR:
FINANCIAL PLANNING FOR ALL AGES 15

CHAPTER FIVE:
BUILDING WEALTH 21

CHAPTER SIX:
WHY I'M NOT WILD ABOUT MUTUAL FUNDS 25

CHAPTER SEVEN:
COMMON INVESTOR MISTAKES 29

CHAPTER EIGHT:
FIDUCIARY DUTY 31

CHAPTER NINE:
KNOW THE RISK OF YOUR INVESTMENTS 37

CHAPTER TEN:
LIFE INSURANCE IS NOT AN INVESTMENT 41

CHAPTER ELEVEN:
SEQUENCE OF RETURNS 47

CHAPTER TWELVE:
ALTERNATIVE INVESTMENTS 55

CHAPTER THIRTEEN:
FIXED INDEXED ANNUITIES 59

CHAPTER FOURTEEN:
PROTECTING AGAINST ELDER ABUSE 65

CHAPTER FIFTEEN:
SO TAXING 69

CHAPTER SIXTEEN:
PLANNING FOR LONG-TERM CARE 75

CHAPTER SEVENTEEN:
MASS PRODUCTION: IS IT RIGHT FOR YOUR PORTFOLIO? 81

CHAPTER EIGHTEEN:
STRUCTURED NOTES 85

CHAPTER NINETEEN:
THE FINAL CHAPTER 89

CHAPTER TWENTY:
THINKING BIG PICTURE? 93

ABOUT THE AUTHOR 95

INTRODUCTION

The Life You Deserve

Most of the time, with some occasional but noteworthy exceptions, people get pretty much what they deserve, based on the choices they have made throughout their lives.

When it comes to accumulating wealth, people who make smart, educated, disciplined choices tend to be more successful than people who have been unable to learn how to make the right choices consistently. If you were always a good saver who lives within your means, you are likely on your way to financial independence or have already achieved it. You probably feel a strong sense of financial security and low stress at least as it relates to money. However, financial independence will only remain for those who continue to make smart choices.

Conversely, those who make poor choices generally suffer the consequences. If you have chosen to live beyond your means and you haven't been a disciplined investor, you are likely less wealthy than you could have been. Similarly, if you haven't created written goals and a plan to achieve those goals, you may not have achieved the kind of financial success you wanted. You may feel a degree of anxiety about being able to achieve your financial goals or perhaps if you are already retired, you may fear running out of money. If you haven't made optimal choices about the planning and eventual distribution of your assets at death, the legacy you desire could be at risk.

Regardless of your stage in life, whether you're independently wealthy or not sure if you can retire and not run out of money, it's probably not too late to increase your level of abundance simply by making better choices. Whether it's changing your spending habits or making better investment choices, or educating yourself on the latest financial strategies, there almost always exists an opportunity to obtain the life that you deserve.

I've written this book to help you do just that.

CHAPTER ONE

The Law of Giving

"No one has ever become poor by giving." Anne Frank

Chances are if you're reading this book, one of your goals is to find strategies that will increase your abundance. That abundance provides the ability to do what you want, live where you want, and go where you want without having to worry about money. Most people would like to be in that position. This book was written to help you make smart choices about your money. Whether you are trying to grow your investments, create income, or leave a large legacy, I will discuss various techniques to help achieve those goals.

Before we explore those, however, you will want to make sure that you are doing all the things you must to maintain a life of wealth and abundance. Have you ever met anyone who had acquired significant wealth, yet did not seem to be highly intelligent or possess any special qualities that would seemingly be indicative of one who had the ability to acquire significant wealth? On the flipside, we all probably know some very intelligent people who can't seem to find financial success. I think about this paradox frequently. I have spent a lot of time trying to understand this apparent disconnect.

Once upon a time, I faced my fair share of financial adversity. In 1999, I was broke. Actually, that's not accurate. I was so far in debt that my goal was just to get back to broke. How did I get in that position? After graduating from law school with honors, I practiced law for a few years before transitioning into financial services in 1996 with a large, well-known company. I did very well, very quickly. After my first year, I was recognized by my company at its annual meeting as one of their rising stars.

I was impressed with myself, but I quickly received a lesson in humility. My first son, Jake, was born in late 1998. We had just bought a bigger house. We went from being a two-income family to a one-income family. We also had hired a nanny. Expenses were way up, and revenue was down. Each month I was facing a shortfall. Credit card debt was starting to mount. By the time Jake celebrated his first birthday, I was getting close to running out of credit. If you have ever been in the position of not knowing whether you would have enough money at the end of the month to meet all your family's financial obligations, you would know how stressed I was.

I was extremely worried and frustrated. Why did I have so little abundance and so much scarcity even though I was extremely intelligent and highly educated? This question consumed me. I was determined to learn how to bring abundance to my life. If other people could have abundance, all I needed to do was learn their methods and replicate them. I started to read voraciously about how to obtain abundance. One book that influenced me greatly was the *Seven Spiritual Laws of Success* by Deepak Chopra. I learned that whatever you want to receive, you must give. If you want love, you must give love. If you want to be blessed with abundance, you must try to help others obtain abundance. That means I needed to focus on helping as many people as possible become abundant.

In times of distress, it's not uncommon for people to turn to religion. As someone looking for answers, I was no exception. I started to study the key principles of my faith. Through my religious studies, I learned about the duty to help those who are less fortunate and tithe 10 percent of one's pay to charitable causes. I was ready to do what it took to bring abundance into my life. Everything that I was learning told me that I needed to be more generous if I wanted a better life. I was determined to do what was necessary.

Although I was running out of credit, I borrowed $1,800 around the end of 1999 and donated it to a charity for abused and neglected children. It was the single best financial decision that I have ever made. My life changed almost instantly. My business took off. I was able to pay off all my debt within a year. Today I am blessed to be able to donate six figures each year to worthy charitable causes. My hope is that my business can continue to grow to increase the amount that I give to charities exponentially.

I have become certain that one way to become wealthier in all aspects of your life is to be more generous. Keep in mind, however, that giving reluctantly will not result in abundance. I'm also not implying that if you donate, you will automatically have great financial success. The mindset behind one's giving is critical. According to *The Seven Spiritual Laws of Success*, "The intention behind our giving and receiving is the most important factor. When giving is joyful, when it is unconditional, and from the heart, then the energy behind the giving increases many times over. But if we give grudgingly, there is no energy behind that giving. If we feel we have lost something through the act of giving, then the gift is not truly given and will not cause increase." In other words, you must give to others with joy and not out of obligation.

Here are some tips for putting the law of giving into effect: Obviously, charitable donations are great, but giving doesn't have to be in the form of cash. You can give a non-material gift to everyone that you encounter. It can be a compliment, a friendly gesture, or even a silent prayer. Also, acts of kindness such as paying for someone's coffee, leaving a thoughtful note around the house, or complimenting a stranger are all great random acts of generosity. If you become more generous, you will often find that those around you and even the entire universe might just reciprocate. Even if you have no apparent means to increase your income, it does not matter. Somehow, in some way, good things will happen. Increasing your giving will undoubtedly keep goodness circulating in your life. But, remember to gratefully receive all gifts you are offered because if you aren't willing to accept what the universe gives you, the flow of abundance will dry up. By continuing to both give and receive joy and gratitude, you will keep abundance in your life.

CHAPTER TWO

"I Don't Need Anyone's Help"

"**W**hy should I use a financial advisor?"

It's a good question, and something anyone serious about taking care of their financial future should ask. While some people have a knack for investing, research clearly shows that, over time, the average mutual fund investor, significantly underperforms the overall returns of both stock and bond indexes.[1] This underperformance is largely due to poor market timing decisions.

Vanguard, widely regarded as the leader in offering investment choices for do-it-yourself investing, conducted a study and learned a financial advisor could add three percentage points to a client's investment returns each year. The study found five ways advisors can add value to a client's performance:[2]
- Behavioral coaching
- Asset Location
- Spending Strategy
- Cost-Effective Implementation
- Rebalancing

Vanguard's study revealed the biggest deterrents to individual investor returns are the allure of market timing and the temptation to chase performance. Advisors can help you stick to your investing plan in good times and bad. That means not exiting the market during a correction such as the credit crisis or getting too excited about fads such as the tech bubble.

---

[1] Dana Anspach. The Balance. August 28, 2020. "Why Average Investors EEarn Below Average Market Returns." https://www.thebalance.com/why-average-investors-earn-below-average-market-returns-2388519

[2] Francis Kinniry; Colleeen Jaconetti; Michael DiJoseph; Yan Zilbering; Donald Bennyhoff. Vanguard. February 2019. "Putting a Value on Your Value: Quantifying Vanguard Advisor's Alpha." https://www.vanguard.com/pdf/ISGQVAA.pdf

Advisors can help you construct optimal portfolio balance by attempting to minimize the impact taxes will have by holding the right asset classes in taxable and tax-deferred accounts. If you have multiple tax-deferred and taxable accounts, an advisor can help you devise a withdrawal strategy designed to minimize the tax impact and extend the longevity of your portfolio.

Studies have shown low-cost mutual funds deliver more to shareholders than high-cost mutual funds over long periods.[3] Advisors can point you toward low-cost active funds or index funds that could help increase your overall portfolio value over the long term. Reviewing your portfolio regularly to rebalance your investment strategy is a good way to help reduce risk, Vanguard's study showed.

I'm reminded of a surgeon I first contacted in 1999. I'll call him Danny to keep his identity anonymous. He was living in South Florida but was originally from my hometown. When I got to his office, I inquired about his current planning and investments. His wife was trading their accounts, he said, and she was doing so well that he was contemplating early retirement. His wife would call him every day, he said, and excitedly tell him how much she had made that day. It was not uncommon for her to make $20,000 to $50,000 per day trading tech stocks. Naturally, I counseled him about the need to be more conservative. Like most people who had been watching their accounts steadily appreciate, however, it was very hard to convince them that their strategy was flawed.

Three years later, I reviewed notes gathered about prospective clients I had met with when the stock markets had been surging. I came across my notes with Dr. Danny.

"Hello, Doctor. How have you been? How is your wife making out with her trading?"

This was a loaded question. I already knew the answer as the tech markets had crashed.

"Unfortunately, things started going really bad," Dr. Danny replied. "My wife lost a lot of money and she's very depressed about it."

He agreed to meet with me and revisit our conversation from a few years earlier. He and his wife hired me to become their advisor.

I saw something similar happen in my own family. My grandfather

---

[3] Jean Folger. Investopedia. May 5, 2019. "Pay Attention to Your Fund's Expense Ratio." https://www.investopedia.com/articles/personal-finance/092613/pay-attention-your-funds-expense-ratio.asp

was able to grow a $200,000 nest egg into $1 million by investing in five tech stocks. After he died, I counseled my grandmother, "I think you're taking too much risk by being so heavily invested in tech stocks." She decided to sell half of the tech portfolio and put that money into long-term government bonds.

My uncles were upset: "Why are you selling your stocks? They're doing so good!"

I was quite proud of my grandmother for taking prudent action to diversify before the tech crash, even as my uncles balked at the idea. But how many people who rode the tech stock boom saw their portfolios decimated because they didn't invest wisely?

In a 2018 column called "You Suck at Investing – But it's Not Your Fault," Robert Baharian lists five common cognitive biases that torpedo investors:[4]

1. A tendency to anchor on the first piece of information you receive when making decisions
2. Recency bias, or the tendency to place too much value on the most recent information available, because it is the freshest
3. A tendency to dislike losing much more than they enjoy winning; this "loss aversion" leads to a lot of inaction
4. Bandwagon behavior, or a tendency to do things because many others are doing the same thing
5. Confirmation bias or sticking with information that confirms our own point of view and rejecting anything that conflicts with it

If you think about it, we are all wired as humans to avoid danger. People who lacked that instinct often died because they failed to avoid dangerous situations. Through natural selection, people who lacked the impulse to avoid danger died out, and the people who had developed the instinct to avoid danger survived and passed that trait on. Generally, people that are here today are here because their ancestors developed the ability to avoid danger. Whenever we read the headlines about the latest economic crisis and we see the stock market falling, we immediately sense impending danger. Our instincts scream, "Sell!" our stocks and flee to safety. Moreover, in my experience, many of us have many other biases that contribute to poor investment decisions.

The results can mean a cavalcade of investing missteps: buying or

---

[4] Robert Baharian. LinkedIn. April 29, 2018. "You Suck at Investing—But It's Not Your Fault." https://www.linkedin.com/pulse/you-suck-investing-its-your-fault-robert-baharian

selling at the wrong time, hanging onto losing trades, or missing opportunities because of preconceived notions of the price. You may be convinced that you're not just anyone that you're smarter than the average investor. But trading stories are like fish stories. They're bigger and better in the imagination than they are in real life.

Some advisors, including this author, will also provide their clients with attractive investment strategies that they were either not aware of or would not otherwise have accessed. Many alternative strategies are available aside from the traditional stock and bond allocations, which can potentially enhance an investor's overall portfolio. I will be discussing some of those strategies in subsequent chapters.

A financial advisor can help you stay grounded, identify and counter your biases, and help your investment portfolio achieve your goals. Now, let's get started.

CHAPTER THREE

From Solving Problems to Preventing Them

When I meet with a new prospective client, it's not unusual for the same question to come up.

"Why did you transition from being a lawyer to being a financial adviser?" I will typically relate the following story from when I was a young attorney.

In one of my first cases, a woman came to me after her mother had recently died.

"I think my sister might have stolen the inheritance," she told me.

Her mother had about $400,000 saved up. My new client lived in Philadelphia, her mother had been living in Florida since she retired, and her sister lived in Oklahoma. My client's mother had a pension from the federal government that comfortably paid all her bills. But when she reached a point where she could no longer take care of herself, she decided to move to a nursing home in Tulsa to be near the daughter who lived there. Like most parents, she intended to leave her assets equally among her children. She hired an attorney to draft a will, in which she left her assets to both daughters in equal shares. My client's mother lived in the nursing home for a couple of years in Oklahoma with no real contact with the outside world except her daughter who lived in Oklahoma, and her other daughter, my client, who lived in Philadelphia. My client's sister took control of her mother's finances as she lost the capacity to run her own affairs.

When my client's mother died, the funeral was held in Florida, where she had purchased a burial plot next to her husband. After the funeral, my client's sister casually informed her that there "was nothing left". My client was shocked to hear that. Based on her knowledge of her mother's finances, that did not seem plausible. Her understanding was that her mother's monthly pension should have been enough to pay for the nursing home's annual cost. Therefore, her estimated savings of about $400,000 should have been intact. My client's sister was not willing to provide any financial documentation. There was no power of attorney and no revocable trust.

The first thing we needed to do was get the bank records to see what happened to the savings. The bank would not provide my client any records because she had no prior authorization. We needed to subpoena the records, but we first needed to open a probate estate to do that. At that time, we didn't even have a copy of the will. I went to Oklahoma, opened an intestacy estate claiming that we did not possess a copy of the will. Once the probate estate was opened, I was able to have a subpoena issued, which compelled the bank to provide us with the records. Those records showed that my client's sister had put her name on the account while their mother was still alive to "help manage the bills." It turned out that my client's sister was truthful when she stated that there was nothing left. Prior to her death, my client's sister wrote herself a check for $400,000 to her own checking account. Therefore, there were no assets to even probate as her mother technically died penniless.

Our only option was to file a lawsuit for fraud and civil theft against her sister. At the trial, the sister claimed that her mother, even in her diminished mental capacity, had "wanted" her to have all the money since she was the one taking care of her. Unfortunately, this is a very common fact pattern. There was simply no evidence that my client's mother had intended to disinherit her at the eleventh hour. It was a classic case of elder abuse.

As we expected, the judge ruled in our favor. He cited the fact that there was no change in the will and no tax returns documenting the gift. He awarded half of the money to my client.

When you go into a nursing home, I believe that you become susceptible to suggestion a lot more than when you are self-sufficient. Elder abuse comes mostly from relatives or people close to you – often kids who feel entitled for whatever reason to more of the money than others.[5]

I can relate to those who have seen their loved ones being taken advantage of because my client in the case I just recounted was my mother. We had to sue my aunt to get half of the money, as specified by

---

[5] J. Peterson, D. Burnes, P. Caccamise, A. Mason, C. Henderson, M. Wells, and M. Lachs. *Journal of General Internal Medicine*. 2014. "Financial exploitation of older adults: a population-based prevalence study." 29(12), 1615–23. doi: 10.1007/s11606-014-2946-2

her mother's will. To this day, we don't talk to my aunt or my cousin. I am sure that was not the legacy my grandmother wanted to leave. She just did not plan it correctly. She did not put safeguards in place, such as getting dual power of attorney instead of putting her daughter's name on the account.

I realized that, as an attorney, I could help people try to fix problems. As a Certified Financial Planner™ professional and financial advisor, I could help people prevent problems. That is why I became a financial advisor and CFP in addition to continuing my estate planning practice. My legal experience combined with my financial planning expertise allows me to help our clients efficiently manage their assets and assist them in getting optimal outcomes for themselves and their families.

CHAPTER FOUR

Financial Planning for All Ages

As a Certified Financial Planner™ professional and financial advisor with over twenty-five years of experience, I have worked with people in many stages of their lives. Depending on where they are in their lives, my advice will vary widely. Many people don't start the financial planning process early enough. Even grade school children can learn to budget. Instead of giving your child money whenever they need it, try giving a fixed amount each week so that they learn about saving and budgeting. The earlier they learn that they shouldn't be spending every cent they get, the better.

When I was in the second grade, lunch at Philadelphia public schools cost 60 cents. It usually included a main course like chicken, fish, or a hamburger. It also included a vegetable, dessert, and a carton of milk. We were given a "spork," a plastic spoon/fork combined into one, as our utensil. Anyway, one Monday morning on my way to school my father didn't have exact change, so he gave me a $5 bill and he said, "This is for the whole week." On that Monday, I purchased the 60-cent lunch "platter." However, the cafeteria also sold other things like chocolate chip cookies and brownies, which were delicious. I had "extra" money, so I purchased them not only for myself but my friends too. After all, I am an exceptionally good friend. The same thing happened on Tuesday and Wednesday. Although I was very popular with my friends, I was out of money by Wednesday. When I asked my dad for more money on Thursday morning, he was not happy, to say the least. "What happened?? I gave you more than enough money." While it was true that he gave me more than enough resources to afford lunch every day without running out of money, he never gave me a plan on how to budget the money. In my experience, the same is true of many successful adults. They make more than enough income to afford food, shelter, clothing, healthcare, transportation, education for their children, and a comfortable retirement. Yet because of poor planning, poor investment strategies, and a lack of discipline, many fail to achieve their goals.

In my case, my failure to get good advice and plan correctly would have caused me to drastically reduce my standard of living had my father not chosen to bail me out. Unfortunately, most of us do not have a benefactor who gives us money to fix our financial mistakes. Luckily, I was still young enough to learn from and ultimately recover from my first financial setback. From that point on, I learned to save my money. I sold soft pretzels in front of my father's appliance store in Northeast Philadelphia. I also worked most summers at a hot dog stand and as a busboy in different restaurants. I even started my own house cleaning business the summer after college. While I had learned to save and live below my means, I still had no long-term financial plan, which identified my goals and objectives and a way to achieve those goals. In 1995 while I was a 28-year old practicing attorney, a financial planner whom I was friendly with asked me to meet with him.

At this point, I had obtained a finance degree, a law degree, and I had accumulated a modest brokerage account. I didn't necessarily feel as if I needed a financial planner. Because I knew him, I felt that I would give him the courtesy of a meeting. At our meeting, the planner asked me some basic questions. "Keith, what are some of your life goals? What are some of your financial goals? What are you doing for your eventual retirement? What would you do to support yourself if you got sick or hurt and you couldn't work?" I didn't have a good answer for most of his questions. These questions made me feel very uncomfortable because they made me realize that I was not making proper financial choices. He had opened my eyes to the fact that not only didn't I have a good financial plan, but I also wasn't able to readily articulate my goals. I quickly realized that if someone who was trained in finance and had been investing since he was 16 didn't have a good financial plan, then many other people similarly probably did not have a good financial plan. A lot of people needed assistance in this area. This realization was another one of the factors which led me to my transition from attorney to Financial Planner.

Before people start making money after they complete their education, there usually isn't much planning. However, once one starts their first full-time job, they should set both short- and long-term goals and start the financial planning process. Someone who is just starting out has different goals than someone who is either in or near retirement. Typically, someone who just started their career has very few assets to manage. However, they do have an extended earning capacity ahead of them that they need to correctly manage. In fact, their future earning capacity is by far their most valuable asset. Therefore, it is important to protect that asset. According to the Social Security Administration, more than one in four of today's twenty-year-olds can expect to be out of work for at least a year because of a disabling condition before they reach the normal retirement age.[6] Therefore, it's highly advisable that people who are working consider acquiring a long-term disability income insurance policy. As a young planner, I typically wound up working with my contemporaries. I regularly recommended disability income insurance, although most people weren't excited about paying for it. However, over the years, I did have a few clients that became disabled and those policies helped save them from financial distress. They are deeply grateful that I suggested that they own the appropriate coverage.

Once one's most valuable asset is protected, people need to accumulate wealth for various reasons. Retirement, purchasing a home, starting a business, or paying for children's education are all accumulation goals. If you add up all a younger person's future goals, they probably aren't making enough to save everything they need to achieve their goals. That's not an insurmountable problem because most people typically see their annual income increase over time. One of the best things a financial planner can do is to get their clients to embark on a systematic savings program as soon as possible and keep increasing it as often as possible. The power of compounding over long periods of time can be beneficial for those trying to accumulate wealth. Starting early is crucial to giving yourself the greatest opportunity to reach your financial goals.

If someone waits until they are 40 to start saving $800 per month for retirement, they will have $611,575 at age 67 if they earn 6 percent per year in returns. However, if that person had started saving $500 per month at age thirty, they would have $763,575 at age 67, even though they contributed less each month. The sooner you start, the more time your money will have to grow—and the better the opportunity you will have to reach your goals.

The retirement plan at work is often an ideal place for many people to start systematically saving money. Still, for many people, even "maxing it out" your retirement account not going to create sufficient wealth to meet all of one's financial goals. Moreover, not everyone has

---

[6] Social Security Administration. 2020. "Disability Facts." https://www.ssa.gov/disabilityfacts/facts.html.

access to a work-sponsored plan. In my opinion, IRA contribution limits are not high enough for most people to achieve their retirement goals. Most people need to save additional funds on their own. The one thing most younger workers have going for them is a long-term time horizon. They don't need to be able to spend their retirement savings for decades. That means for people in that stage of life. I would tend to recommend mostly stock-based investments. They don't need to stress as much about stock market crashes because they have plenty of time to hopefully recover. In fact, during stock market crashes, long-term systematic savers can benefit because when they add more money to their accounts, as they are buying their investments at lower prices. Long-term retirement savers will have more money in their accounts (provided they remain invested) if there are periodic corrections followed by big recoveries than if the markets consistently and steadily rise.

For those who are about to retire or who are already retired, my advice would be much different. This is their only nest egg. Therefore, we need to use risk mitigation strategies that help reduce the risk of loss. People who are no longer working do not have the same time horizons as they did twenty years earlier. Moreover, corrections are harmful for people who are no longer adding to their accounts and instead are taking money out to live each month. One should also develop an income plan to determine how to create the necessary income to maintain their lifestyle tax-efficiently. Therefore, for many people in retirement, I typically recommend strategies designed to reduce volatility—otherwise, they could potentially suffer from sequence of returns risk. This is when investors are forced to take money out of their investments when they are down. One exception to this general rule is that if you do not need to take income from your investment accounts because you have sufficient income from pensions or other assets, then you may be able to maintain a larger exposure to stocks even if you are retired. In that case, the investments continue to have a longer-term time horizon. Unlike their younger working counterparts, the most valuable asset for many retirees is their savings and investment portfolios. In that circumstance, one of the most important objectives is conservation. Just like younger workers must acquire insurance to protect their most valuable asset, retirees also need to consider owning insurance to help protect their nest egg. One such insurance is called long-term care insurance. We discuss this in greater detail later in the book, but for many people, an extended time needing long-term care is the one curveball that could derail their retirement. The potential cost must be planned for in any case. In summary, younger people need to start their planning as soon as possible, save as much as possible, and understand the importance of investing for growth. As people approach retirement, they need to adjust their portfolios to account for a potentially shorter time horizon before needing their money and create a portfolio with less volatility so that it may withstand significant market drawdowns that will periodically occur.

CHAPTER FIVE

Building Wealth

I often tell people there are three ways to become wealthy: through a fortuitous event like an inheritance or lottery, through the growth of a successful business which creates large annual cash flow or a significant liquidity event, or by utilizing a systematic savings strategy from one's income. The last method is the only one that's not tenuous, in my opinion.

Systematic savings can be extremely effective. Many people who work for a company are doing that by contributing to their employer-sponsored retirement plan. I meet people who are about to retire and the only real savings they have is what they contributed systematically into their work retirement plan. The remaining paycheck they spent on their lifestyle. They got used to living on that amount of money. As their income increased, so did their lifestyle. People quickly get used to living on their take-home pay. Have you ever been foreclosed on or had your vehicle repossessed? Probably not. The reason that doesn't happen is because you know you must make those payments.

People tend to figure out that if they have a certain amount of income, they can afford a certain amount for housing and other basic living expenses. When people decide to allocate a portion of their income to savings each month, they start to build wealth even if they blow all the rest of their paycheck. Conversely, if you don't make regular systematic payments to your savings and investments, you might look up one day and realize you don't have the life you wanted. You may not be able to afford to retire or send a child to college or travel and enjoy your leisure time. You must make it mandatory in the same way you pay your mortgage, your car loan, and your electric bill. It must become a habit, not something you do every now and then.

If your employer offers a 401(k) or Roth IRA, think about signing up and begin making regular contributions. Most companies can withdraw your contribution directly from your paycheck, so you never see the money. Many offer matching contributions up to a certain percentage. I know it can be hard to save money when you're first starting out, particularly if you have student loan debt, but I suggest you at least find a way to capture your employer's matching contribution. Otherwise, you're simply throwing away free money. If your employer doesn't offer a 401(k), perhaps you can set up an individual Roth IRA and make regular contributions—whether it's every paycheck, every month, or every quarter. Some financial advisers even suggest establishing a Roth IRA in addition to a 401(k). Contributions to a 401(k) are made pre-tax, which means you'll pay taxes on withdrawals later. Contributions to Roth IRAs are made after taxes, so you won't be taxed when pulling money out for qualified withdrawals.

One of the hidden advantages of having those contributions withdrawn from your paycheck is you never see the money, which means you can't spend it on impulse buys like a cappuccino or dinner at the latest trendy restaurant. Those purchases add up. Before you know it, you're treading water financially. Curbing those purchases is just one step in taking a closer look at where you're spending your money. Chances are, you'll find areas where you can reduce that spending and redirect it toward investments or long-term goals.

The sooner you're able to start setting money aside for retirement, the greater the opportunity for reward down the road. Albert Einstein called compound interest "the most powerful force in the universe." He's also credited with calling it "the eighth wonder of the world." Compound interest is interest added to the principal of a sum so that the added interest also earns interest from then on. That process, called compounding, helps sums to grow more rapidly over time.

Generally, your investment strategies should be modified relative to where you are in life. When you're young and building wealth, it's usually ideal to be more aggressive in stocks, equities, and exchange-traded funds. ETFs, often called index funds, can also be an effective, low-cost way to diversify your portfolio. As you earn raises and promotions and your earning power increases, you should increase your systematic savings as well. Again, it boils down to the power of compound interest. The more you can take advantage of compound interest, and the sooner you get started, the better off you're likely to be down the road.

I believe that younger investors—in their 20s and 30s—should take as much risk as they can handle, as much as their personal risk tolerance allows. With decades before retirement, there is plenty of time to potentially overcome downturns in the market, and the higher potential reward that typically comes with riskier investments could lead to better long-term returns. Bear in mind, not all investing has to be for retirement. You may want to start saving money toward your children's education or nice vacations, or a second home. Whatever your goals, the key is to start as soon as you can.

By the time you reach your 40s, investing for your retirement should take priority. You still have time to make up lost ground if you started late or were limited in how much you could contribute as a result of other financial obligations. If you have bounced from job to job over the years and have multiple 401(k) accounts, you can roll them over and consolidate them into an individual retirement account. This can help you avoid early withdrawal penalties that come with 401(k)s. IRAs also offer access to more investment options, allowing you to customize your portfolio and build in more diversity. With diversity comes more protection against sudden plunges in the market[7].

If you haven't met with a financial planner yet, your 40s are a wise time to do it. A planner can provide a picture of your financial health and ways to best get where you want to be given your future earnings, expenses, spending, inflation, and any other issues that may enter the picture. Debt reduction usually moves to center stage in your fifties, while you still have what should be peak earning power. Be careful about taking on new debt because you will have less time to pay it off—especially if you want to build your retirement nest egg at the same time.

By the time your fifties arrive, you likely see some significant changes in your life. You may well have children in or on their way to college and you've hit your peak earning years. Depending on how much of your children's post-secondary educations you are helping to finance, this could be the ideal time to ramp up your efforts to save for retirement. If you've maxed out your 401(k) plan at work, you can supplement it with an IRA. Regulations allow for additional "catch-up contributions" of as much as $6,000 a year for your 401(k) and $1,000 a year for your IRA.

Building up your retirement savings should be your first priority at this point, but it's also wise to start paying down your debts. Pay down the ones costing you the most first. That's typically credit card debt, which can be consolidated on lower-interest cards. Money not going toward debts can go toward your retirement savings. With less time

---

[7] Diversification does not ensure a profit or guarantee against losses.

before retirement now available, it's wise to manage your risk. Someone in their mid-fifties has less time to recover from a downturn in the market than a person in their mid-thirties. If you're heavily invested in stocks, it might be wise to consider more conservative investments. While the returns will likely be lower, they'll help reduce your risk due to market loss.

As you reach your sixties, you know more than you ever have and you're wiser than you've ever been. You can use those strengths to explore opportunities to launch side ventures that can augment your late-career income and pare down debts or boost your retirement savings. It's never too late to save for retirement—or even pursue your dreams. Harland Sanders and Grandma Moses are just two examples of people whose fortunes and impact didn't blossom until they had reached their mid-sixties or beyond. In short, it's never too late to add to your nest egg if the opportunity and your health allow it.

CHAPTER SIX

Why I'm Not Wild About Mutual Funds

Mutual funds are a bedrock of many an investor's portfolios, and they've been around in one form or another for centuries, so it may surprise you to hear that I think investing in them may not your best option.

Before I get into why I'm not generally a fan, let me offer some background on mutual funds. They were created in response to a financial crisis that crippled Europe in the 1770s. The British East India Company had borrowed vast sums to finance its colonial interests, especially in North America. While ambitions rose, revenues fell, and the resulting bail-out by the British government left repercussions felt around the world.

Similar pressures emerged in Holland, as efforts to expand its colonial empire piled up huge debts. Historians say Dutch merchant Adriaan van Ketwich came up with the idea to pull together money from several people to form an investment trust – widely considered the world's first mutual fund – in 1774. Small investors were the fund's primary supporters, and risk was reduced by diversifying acquisitions in the American colonies and throughout Europe. The fund owned bonds issued by foreign governments and plantation loans in the West Indies. Income from those plantations helped back the investments, mirroring modern mortgage-backed securities. Only 2,000 shares were created in the closed-end fund that Van Ketwich called "Eendraft Maakt Magt," and participation in the fund was only available to those who bought shares from current shareholders in the open market. Soon, two more funds were established, also relying on diversification to help reduce risk. One fund created by Van Ketwich would last for 114 years before being dissolved.

What is widely considered the first official investment trust – the Foreign and Colonial Government Trust – was founded in London in 1868, and shares of the fund are still traded on the London Stock Exchange today. A generation later, the Boston Personal Property Trust in 1893 became the first closed-end fund – meaning only a designated number of shares was created - launched in America.

Not long after that, the Alexander Fund was established, becoming the first to allow investors to withdraw money on demand. Because of that feature, historians commonly describe the Alexander as the first modern mutual fund. The Roaring Twenties saw a surge in mutual funds, in line with a booming market investors thought would never end.

But we all know what happened. Black Friday in 1929 sent markets crashing around the world and the Great Depression crippled the mutual fund industry. Several measures passed as part of the New Deal brought safeguards designed to protect investors: the creation of the Securities and Exchange Commission, the Securities Act of 1933, and the Securities Exchange Act of 1934. Those steps created a watchdog agency and required quarterly filings and made a prospectus available to investors.

Mutual funds didn't surge again until the post-war boom of the 1950s. By 1951, more than 100 mutual funds were active and that figure more than doubled over the next two decades. Aggressive growth funds were developed in the 1960s, gambling on the performance of high-tech stocks. The index fund – which holds all the stocks of a particular market measure – was introduced in 1971 by Wells Fargo. But it was Vanguard that made the index fund memorable by creating the First Index Investment Trust. Based on the Standard & Poors 500 Index, it was made available to retail investors, meaning Mom and Pop investors could buy shares in the nation's blue-chip, publicly traded companies.

Much of the growth in individual investing was powered by the creation of Individual Retirement Accounts and 401(k) accounts, which replaced traditional pensions at many companies. This allowed people from all walks of life to invest, typically in mutual funds.

The next revolution in investment vehicles arrived in 1993 when the Standard & Poor's Depository Receipts fund was created. Dubbed

SPDRs, or "spiders," it was based on the S&P 500 Index. Over the years, low-cost Exchange Traded Funds, or ETFs, have also been available as well and have the potential to perform as well or better than actively managed stock funds.

Although mutual funds have a long and eventful history, I rarely recommend them to my clients.

For one thing, while past performance isn't indicative of future results, Dalbar, a financial research firm, has consistently found in its report of investor behavior that most mutual funds provide lower returns than their market benchmarks. This difference only widens over time. In the first four months of 2020, 64 percent of actively managed U.S. stock funds lagged the performance of S&P 500 index funds. Over a fifteen-year period, that gap widens to 88 percent of actively managed U.S. funds.[8] This performance gap is exacerbated by the fund fees, which aren't always transparent. All mutual funds cost money to run, pay their managers and employees as well as the usual office and marketing expenses.

On top of that mutual funds exist to make a profit. To that extent, the fund charges investors annual expenses published in the prospectus as an overall percentage of assets and is called the expense ratio. These fees could run from less than a half of a percent per year to over two percent per year, depending on the fund company and the type of fund. Additionally, mutual funds also incur trading costs when they buy and sell stocks in their fund. These trading costs are not published in the prospectus, and according to a study by Elden, Evans and Kadlec the trading costs could average about 1.44 percent per year on top of the expense ratio. Furthermore, many funds have high turnover, which could result in annual tax liability for the fund holders, even those who haven't sold any shares. Finally, many funds keep a good amount of cash on hand to meet redemptions from shareholders, and this typically acts as a

---

[8] Karen Langley. *The Wall Street Journal.* June 10, 2020. "Stock Pickers Underperformed During Coronavirus Market Turmoil."
https://www.wsj.com/articles/stock-pickers-underperformed-during-coronavirus-market-turmoil-11591786801.

drag on performance. Always remember, the higher the fees, the higher return you'll require to make any kind of gains.

These numbers are one of the reasons why I often recommend low-cost ETFs over mutual funds to my clients.

CHAPTER SEVEN

Common Investor Mistakes

You may consider yourself a savvy investor, staying on top of the latest trends and perhaps even outperforming your friends and neighbors in the market. But research has shown that the average active equity fund investor often underperforms the S&P 500—and by a substantial margin.[9]

All too often, those decisions are mistakes. Here are some of the more common blunders:

Recency bias — Giving too much weight to the most recent information available because that's what is freshest in our minds. That often leads to buying stocks that have been going up and selling stocks that have been dropping, because recency bias suggests those trends will only continue. But those emotionally charged decisions can erode earnings potential by leading the investor to hold onto a stock too long or getting out too soon.

Feeling the need to do…something — Unless they're nearing retirement, wise investors maintain a long-term view. But people can get antsy when they see the market have a bad day or a bad week. Selling after a plunge locks in the loss and doesn't give the market an opportunity to rebound. The impulse to try to time the market – another form of "doing something" – is why most investors don't do well on a long-term basis.

Not recognizing your appetite for volatility — Related to the previous point, investors must realize and accept that the market is going

---

[9] Lawrence Carrel. *Forbes.* April 20, 2020. "Passive Management Marks Decade of Beating Active U.S. Stock Funds."
https://www.forbes.com/sites/lcarrel/2020/04/20/passive-beats-active-large-cap-funds-10-years-in-a-row/#222eb27b47b0

to have "corrections" now and then. The point of "enough is enough" is different for every investor and it's important that you know your limits. A good financial adviser can help you figure out what your investment strategy should be, factoring in your tolerance for risk.

Confirmation bias — We see this a lot in society as a whole: people watching cable networks that feature programming consistent with their political leanings or hanging out mostly with people who have similar views. But it can also appear in your investment strategy. Hearing something about a company that confirms your point of view and disregarding anything that conflicts with your beliefs can lead to decisions not based on sound reasoning.

Not knowing where else to go with their money — People often think they're 'diversified' if they have a few different mutual funds. But a truly diverse portfolio will typically combine traditional investments (including high- and low-volatility options), alternative investments such as real estate, commodities or private equity and insurance products such as annuities and life insurance, and perhaps a tactically managed account. Not all investments have to be correlated to the stock market. But be aware of this: most 401(k) plans have limited investment options, so investors may need to use non-retirement assets to balance out their portfolios.

Not paying attention to their personal timeline — The closer you get to retirement, the more you'll need to consider wealth preservation over accumulation. It's critical that you protect the money you'll need for income when your paycheck goes away. It's fine to remain aggressive with some of your funds if you have other assets that will keep income flowing when the market takes a dip. Know that the market will have "corrections" as we go along. If your savings are limited, you should be dialing down the volatility in your portfolio as you get older.

The best way to avoid these mistakes is to make and stick to a financial plan. Knowing where you're going and how you're going to get there can make the journey far less challenging.

Start with strategies that suit your needs. Talk to your adviser and assess the pros and cons. Every time you are tempted to make a change, resist those impulses and stick to your plan.

CHAPTER EIGHT

Fiduciary Duty

There has been a lot of buzz about the word "fiduciary." Certain professions have traditionally acted as fiduciaries to their clients. For instance, doctors are required only to recommend treatments in the best interest of their patients. They owe their patients the duty of loyalty and confidentiality. The same is true for lawyers. If I represent a client as their attorney, I can't represent someone who wants to sue my client. It would be considered a conflict of interest and a breach of my fiduciary duty to do so.

Many other relationships do not rise to a fiduciary level. For example, a salesman at a jewelry store does not owe a fiduciary duty to their customers. That is what's known as a buyer-seller relationship. Not only does a salesperson not have to work in your best interest, but he or she is also completely free to sell you a watch for the highest possible price they can get you to pay even if they were willing to sell you the watch for less. When you buy a car, the relationship is not fiduciary. It's borderline adversarial in nature. Both parties are trying to maximize their own outcome. The only real duty owed in a sales relationship is the duty of fair dealing. Even if you are not acting as a fiduciary, you still are not permitted to lie or deceive to consummate a transaction.

Have you ever got a good deal on a car or a watch? If so, you probably didn't think that the car salesman was acting as your fiduciary.

There's nothing wrong with having a buyer-seller relationship, as long as the parties are clear about the nature of the relationship and know what to expect and understand that it's up to them to scrutinize any "advice" for potential lack of objectivity.

A very wise corporate attorney named Mary once called on me to find out about what might be available to her in the life insurance/annuity space for the conservative portion of her portfolio. In the first five minutes of our first meeting, she demanded to know what the nature of our relationship would be if we worked together.

"Are you my fiduciary?"

I was mildly taken aback. No one had ever asked me that before. I responded by giving her a choice. She could hire me to act as her fiduciary and review and explain all the available options, or she could choose a buyer/seller relationship where she would not have to pay me a fee, but I would do the same work as I would under the fiduciary relationship. If she decided to purchase an annuity, I would get compensated by the insurance company.

Mary analyzed my offer and chose the buyer-seller relationship because she could avoid paying my fee out of her pocket. She would still receive the same research as I let her know that I would give her the same recommendations no matter how she chose to compensate me. She also understood that despite my intentions to provide her objective advice, in this instance, I would be subject to a financial bias. I would only receive compensation if she decided to acquire an annuity through my firm. She kept this disclosed fact in the back of her mind when evaluating my recommendations. In this particular transaction, her primary concern was to turn her assets into a legacy for her children and we applied for life insurance. Because of health issues, she was uninsurable, so her second choice was to purchase a fixed index annuity with a guaranteed 8 percent death benefit rider. I agreed it was an attractive option for many but could be especially beneficial to someone who had serious health conditions and wealth transfer objectives. When her health took a turn for the worse, she immediately called me to review her trust and beneficiary designations to ensure that everything would be allocated according to her wishes.

Historically, if you ever worked with a stockbroker, whether you were aware or not, you most likely entered into a buyer-seller relationship. Brokers make commissions in exchange for selling their clients stocks and bonds, and other investments. The more frequently they buy and sell stocks, the more money they make. Brokers were often accused of churning accounts with excessive trades, and they generally were not viewed as fiduciaries. They are called brokers, for goodness' sake, so the parties should know they are salesmen, not fiduciaries. About a year ago, I started working with a client who had been working with a broker at one of the big banks for many years. My new client hadn't been fully satisfied with the relationship or the performance of his account. His broker was making commissions on every recommendation, and he was buying a lot of structured notes because he like the income. I showed him that if he purchased structured notes without the commission that was paid to the broker, he could get substantially better terms as well as higher income on his notes. He asked if he could experience working with our firm with only a portion of his account, at least initially. I agreed and he transferred $250,000 to our management, which represented about 10 percent of his portfolio. After a year, he told me that he felt much better working with an advisor in a fiduciary capacity as opposed to a buyer-seller relationship because of the alignment of mutual interests. So, he moved the rest of his account over to our management.

Because of the negative connotation of being labeled a salesperson, many brokers now use other titles, calling themselves financial consultants or financial advisors. These new titles imply that the broker/financial consultant is no longer a salesman but instead a fiduciary. Yet this isn't often the case and it can be confusing to clients. The important thing for a client or potential client of any advisor is understanding what conflicts of interest they face and understanding those conflicts when evaluating their recommendations. Just being a fiduciary doesn't make one ethical. Conversely, the fact that a salesman gets paid by commission doesn't make them a crook. There are almost always potential conflicts of interest surrounding a financial advisor's revenue and compensation whether they are acting as a fiduciary or a broker.

Many fiduciary advisors attempt to structure their practices to minimize conflicts of interest, but they usually can't eliminate them completely. This conflict applies to all fiduciary professions. For instance, I once broke my finger badly while playing flag football. I consulted with a hand surgeon. He immediately recommended surgery which would require a special metal brace on my hand and arm for eight weeks. It would also be expensive, and he added, "By the way, your finger will never be a hundred percent like it used to be."

Needless to say, this did not sound like an ideal course of action, so I got a second opinion. The second-hand surgeon advised me to wear a splint for eight weeks on my finger, with no expensive surgery and no cumbersome metal cast on my hand and arm. This is the opinion I followed, and I was very pleased with my recovery. I would often think about the doctor who recommended surgery. Did he really believe it was in my best interest, or was he financially motivated to perform surgery? Clearly, there was a financial incentive for him. Perhaps he convinced himself that surgery was necessary. The bottom line is that hand surgeons make a lot of money doing surgery and a relatively small amount recommending finger splints. Although this doctor was supposed to be my fiduciary, his bias of wanting or needing to make more money potentially influenced his advice to me.

Many times, attorneys who represent insurance companies don't settle the cases they are defending until just before the trial. Is it possible they could have reached the same settlement much earlier in the process? Perhaps, but that outcome doesn't help their bottom line, even though they are supposed to be representing their client's best interest.

Financial advisors face the same conflicts even if they are supposed to be acting as your fiduciary. Some advisors have made the business decision not to offer insurance products in their practice. There are a few reasons they may do this. Some advisors have a huge network of sub-advisors across the country, and they need to be able to deliver uniform portfolio models to all their clients across the country. It really would not be feasible to train all their advisors on the constantly changing rates, options, and features of these insurance products and have sufficient quality control over how the final portfolios are constructed. Therefore, it's much easier just to exclude that asset class entirely and offer a few cookie-cutter portfolio choices that can be delivered to the masses. As a local boutique firm, we don't have that problem. We can tailor portfolios to a client's particular situation.

Alternatively, some advisors aren't licensed to offer insurance products, or they have made a business decision not to recommend any product that pays a commission to avoid the appearance of a conflict. That's a choice every financial advisor must make. Do you completely eliminate an entire asset class of products and strategies because you can't trust yourself to be unbiased? Personally, I think the benefit of being able to offer unique solutions with the potential for relatively high risk-adjusted expected returns outweighs any potential conflict.

The commissions paid to agents and advisors for annuities have been dropping considerably over the last decade.[10] For conventionally managed accounts, our firm charges our clients on average about 1 percent each year depending on the account size. We make less revenue recommending annuities over the long run because annuities typically do not pay any annual fees to advisors as they would receive from managing portfolios. In any case, we always do what's in the client's best interest. When there are attractive annuities available, we recommend them and when rates are low and unattractive, we avoid them. Personally, I feel it's a much bigger conflict not having access to an entire class of conservative solutions – based not only on what's available now but what may be available in the future as opposed to having a full toolbox to assist clients.

If a client approaches their advisor who doesn't offer or understand insurance products and asks about a fixed index annuity with solid growth potential and no investment risk, and they don't have to pay a management fee on it, the advisor faces a dilemma. Do they take the time to research the product, knowing that if it turns out to be attractive and the client acquires the product, the adviser will lose revenue since he can't offer it? In some cases, there could be a financial incentive for this so-called impartial fiduciary advisor to tell their client that they would be better off investing the money with the advisor rather than with an insurance company. That isn't necessarily acting in the client's best interests.

---

[10] Scott MacKillop. WealthManagement.com. October 29, 2019. "Op-Ed: Four Reasons Fees Are Dropping Like a Rock—and What It Means for You." https://www.wealthmanagement.com/industry/op-ed-four-reasons-fees-are-dropping-rock-and-what-it-means-you

Many times, to streamline their practice and make their own lives easier, some advisors offer only one or two investment models. Unfortunately, there isn't any model that is exactly what everyone needs at all stages of their lives. Additionally, when a money manager spends millions and millions of dollars buying advertisements trying to convince you to cash in your annuities regardless of your circumstances or the terms of the annuity, that doesn't sound like a fiduciary relationship at all. Regardless of a firm's business model, what matters most is whether an advisor is willing to walk away from revenue or fees if a transaction or recommendation isn't in the client's absolute best interest.

A few years ago, a client referred his friend Richard to me. Richard was unhappy with his variable annuity. Richard explained that another advisor told him his annuity had high fees and he would be better off in a fixed index annuity. He asked my opinion. If he exchanged his annuity, I would stand to earn a considerable commission. After reviewing his variable annuity, I determined that Richard would be able to withdraw 6 percent per year from his variable annuity WITHOUT lowering his guaranteed death benefit. This would essentially work out to be a guaranteed 6 percent return net of all fees with some potential upside on top of that. I recommended that he keep his annuity and not exchange it, and I gave up substantial revenue, but I did what I felt was best for him.

I believe that doing what's best for our clients might cost us money in the short term, but that philosophy makes my firm much more successful in the long run.

SINGER WEALTH ADVISORS DOES ACT AS A FIDUCIARY, but more importantly, we don't make recommendations that aren't in our clients' best interests, even if it means we lose revenue.

CHAPTER NINE

Know the Risk of Your Investments

At the end of 2019, I met with new clients who I will call John and Sarah. They had a few million dollars saved up in their brokerage accounts. They were retired. Both had pensions and Social Security income. They did not have long-term care insurance. Assuming that they didn't have any significant healthcare expenditures, they would only need to take about 3 percent of their portfolio's value each year to maintain their lifestyle. From an estate planning standpoint, they had no kids, and they were leaving all their assets to a few different charities. Their portfolio consisted of thirty different mutual funds, almost all of which invested in the same asset classes. Many of their top holdings within those funds overlapped into eight to ten of the funds each. For instance, they owned the stock Microsoft, but they also owned ten different mutual funds that also owned Microsoft. The portfolio was over-concentrated into a few different sectors of the economy that had done very well.

At our first meeting, they indicated that they wanted to make sure that they would always have enough money to maintain their current lifestyle. Pretty quickly, the conversation turned to risk:

Keith: "What is your risk tolerance?"

John: "I'm moderate to moderate plus."

Sarah: "I'm moderate minus."

Keith: "At this point in your life, if we were going through some economic crisis and the markets started falling, what percentage could you bear to see your account go down before you became so concerned that you might think about selling out of your portfolio?"

John: "I guess about 15-20 percent."

Sarah: "I think for me about 10-15 percent."

I told them that I have a tool that can quickly quantify their risk tolerance and quantify the risk of their portfolio. They went on the following website, www.findoutmyrisk.com, and took a quick survey. This uses software called Riskalyze to measure risk tolerance and the risk of one's portfolio.

John came back at a 70, which means he could tolerate a portfolio consisting roughly of 70 percent diversified equities and 30 percent fixed income. Sarah's risk score was a 58. She was more conservative. A portfolio with a 58-risk score could be expected to drop about 20 percent in value during a major market downturn like the one we had in 2008. The problem with their actual portfolio was that it was grading out at an 83 risk. Their portfolio could go down 40 percent if we got another 2008 type scenario, well beyond the 15 percent they could comfortably handle.

I was noticing several important issues that need to be addressed and resolved. When someone's portfolio is consistently growing over the last decade, they tend to feel pretty good about it. When an investor has been watching their portfolio of "great funds and great stocks" that's "diversified" and consistently appreciating for ten years, they tend to feel that they have a great portfolio. If it ain't broke, don't fix it. The problem with investments is that you won't know if your investment strategy was broken until you lost a bunch of money, unless you have a way to measure the risk in advance, which we do.

I had to explain to John and Sarah that even though their portfolio had been doing well, it was riskier than their comfort level projected. They understood that, but they were hesitant to make major changes because the markets had been doing so well and bonds were paying so little. They were essentially scared of missing out on some additional growth.

I asked them if you doubled your money will you live any differently. They said no. On the other hand, if you lost 40 percent of your money, would that make you nervous about whether you could comfortably maintain your current standard of living? Yes, that would be very stressful. I told them that they were taking the extra risk of getting maximum growth to go to charities eventually. While the charities who are your beneficiaries get 100 percent of the benefit if your aggressive strategies work out, John and Sarah will be the ones who are suffering if we experience a bad market. Does that sound like a good plan? Clearly, it didn't.

If John and Sarah would simply reduce their risk, they could essentially guarantee that they would never run out of money. With the current amount of risk that they were facing, their intended outcome was less certain.

When people are younger and adding to their portfolio, they can afford to be aggressive. Market downturns are the friends of the young systematic investors. Market corrections actually enhance long-term returns because subsequent periodic investments are purchasing additional shares at lower prices. Moreover, younger people are encouraged not to look at their retirement accounts too frequently as they don't need that money any time soon. For many years people are rewarded for having that aggressive mindset, but eventually, things change. They no longer have as much time before they plan to retire. Once they retire, they are no longer contributing to their account. In fact, they are taking money out of their accounts. Therefore, they now need to reevaluate their risk tolerance and the risk tolerance of their portfolio. They need to figure out how to get income. To the extent they have stocks, they need a safe place to pull income from assets other than from the stocks if there is a bad year or two in the market. As you get older, your risk tolerance may not change at all. You may feel very comfortable taking a lot of risk. Arguably degenerate gamblers have a high-risk tolerance. However, everyone also has a risk CAPACITY that is not subjective, and it's completely unrelated to one's risk tolerance. A person worth $100 million certainly has the capacity to risk and lose one million on a speculative investment, but they still may not be willing to tolerate that. Conversely, an aggressive investor with a higher risk tolerance, who has $2,000,000 of investments that need to produce $120,000 per year to support his lifestyle simply cannot afford to lose 40 percent of his portfolio and still maintain his lifestyle. Subjecting his portfolio to that kind of risk is exceeding his risk capacity, even if he is comfortable with an aggressive portfolio. My job is to make sure people do not invest more aggressively than they can tolerate. More importantly, they should not invest more aggressively than they can handle from an economic standpoint.

Many of my clients like knowing that they have set up enough conservative assets to allow them to live their life exactly the way they want with as little risk as possible. For instance, if you can allocate 50 percent of your money to conservative investments that will create all the money you will ever need to meet your financial goals, you can freely invest the rest of the funds aggressively for the long-term benefit of your heirs. In that case, you are investing within your risk capacity. You may still want the rest of your money to be invested conservatively if you have a low-risk tolerance. However, once you have a plan in place that provides you with the assurance that you will never run out of money, you can truly do whatever you want with the remaining funds. Invest it for your beneficiaries or make lifetime gifts to family or charities. Being in this position allows one to have the ultimate financial freedom.

In any case, taking risk is fine as long as it's properly calculated, consistent with your long-term objectives, does not exceed your risk capacity, and is at a level you can emotionally accept when things turn bad. Otherwise, I would advise reducing your risk.

CHAPTER TEN

Life Insurance Is Not an Investment

I often hear various pundits repeat the cliché that life insurance is not an investment. Let's analyze this statement.

According to Investopedia, an investment is an asset or item acquired with the goal of generating income and/or appreciation. Typically, investments have investment risk. For the most part, life insurance does not have any investment risk except for variable life insurance, which isn't widely used, and private placement life insurance, which extremely wealthy families use to shelter their investments from income taxation.

It's estimated that clients of a Blackstone asset management subsidiary placed $3 billion into specially designed investment life insurance contracts to eliminate taxes. Clearly, to the ultra-wealthy, life insurance is not only also an investment but a very tax-savvy investment as well.

Today, you don't have to be ultra-wealthy to own a traditional policy designed for growth and future tax-free income. The operative word there is "design." An experienced advisor should know how to design a life insurance policy to maximize the growth aspect. Most people intuitively want to pay the least amount possible for the most possible death benefit. Therefore, if you design a policy that way, most of the premium will cover the insurance costs. That kind of policy is obviously not designed as an investment. Many people don't realize that if you own a life insurance policy, you can make large premium payments in certain cash value policies. The cash value can grow tax-free. You can also potentially generate significant tax-free income via policy loans and withdrawals. (These withdrawals reduce the cash value and the policy's death benefit and could cause the policy to lapse if you withdraw too much, just like excessive withdrawals could deplete one's investment accounts).

In fact, many insurance companies realized how substantial these tax advantages were in the early 1980s, so they introduced single premium life insurance that had very high cash value potential and very low insurance amounts. When you have low face amounts of insurance, you have lower insurance costs, which can help the cash value grow more quickly. Wealthy investors were using these vehicles essentially as a tax shelter, which had very little resemblance to traditional life insurance policies. The insurance costs were significantly lower than the tax savings. Congress, which blessed life insurance with very favorable tax treatment ostensibly to encourage people to plan correctly and take care of their families, took notice of these contracts and changed the law.

Congress rationalized that the law was not designed to help wealthy people avoid paying taxes. Therefore, in 1988, Congress passed a law called TAMRA, which altered the tax treatment of these single-premium contracts. Post TAMRA, if you try to rapidly overfund a life insurance policy in a single year, your cash value could still grow tax-deferred, the death benefit would still be tax-free, but any withdrawals would be taxable as ordinary income, as well as a potential 10 percent penalty prior to age fifty-nine-and-one-half. These single premium overfunded contracts are known as Modified Endowment Contracts (MECs). They can still be a great choice for someone who was considering a deferred annuity, especially if they don't expect to take a lot of income out of the contracts as all the proceeds at death are tax-free.

Congress created certain stipulations for life insurance products to avoid being taxed as modified endowment contracts. The contracts must be funded over several years, not all at once. In addition, there are limits to how much money can be put into a contract relative to the death benefit. As noted previously, those limits are still fairly high. If designed correctly, the insurance costs, although front-loaded to some extent, typically amount to an average of approximately 1 percent per year of the policy's cash value over longer periods of time.

Most people who invest their money in a brokerage account tend to pay for a financial advisor's input. If you have a financial advisor, you may be paying 1 percent per year of management fees. Although you may pay some insurance costs, you typically don't pay an advisory fee on cash-value life insurance contracts. Moreover, if you use mutual funds, the published expense ratio could be 1 percent per year and the non-published trading costs average about 1.44 percent per year, according to a study published by Forbes.

Finally, traditional investments are not sheltered from taxes. Affluent investors, depending on their state of residence, could be paying over 25 percent taxes on long-term capital gains and over 45 percent taxes on short-term capital gains and interest on their investments. Those figures are based on current tax laws, but they are scheduled to increase in 2026. That means if you earn 10 percent in a year and you must pay 20 percent in taxes, taxes are costing you 20 percent per year of your returns or 2 percent per year of the overall portfolio. I would submit to you that the total cost of ownership between advisory fees, fund fees, trading costs, and taxes on traditional investments can easily be 3 to 5 percent per year.

Another thing to consider is that at least when you pay insurance costs, you actually get life insurance. The last I checked, everyone dies eventually, so your beneficiaries get a death benefit in return for those fees. Whereas paying higher taxes doesn't necessarily earn you any additional government resources.

Moreover, an additional key feature is that you may not even have to die to collect the death benefit. Many contracts now let the policy owner use some of the death benefit tax-free if they need long-term care. Just like with a stand-alone, long-term care policy that pays you a benefit if you can't do two out of six activities of daily living, many life insurance contracts will advance you your death benefit while you are alive if you can no longer take care of yourself or are expected to pass away within the coming year. Costs for additional benefits like long-term care and tax-free death benefit will eventually be recouped when these events occur. According to the federal government, it's estimated that 70 percent of men who reach age sixty-five and 75 percent of women who reach age sixty-five will need some long-term care, so this could be an especially valuable benefit.[11] In my experience, most people don't mind paying a

---

[11] LongTermCare.gov. 2020. "How Much Care Will You Need?"

cost for something as long as the value they get back is greater than the cost.

There are several ways life insurance policies calculate interest. Traditionally, insurers collected premiums and invested them in the company investment portfolios. Because life insurers must manage their investment portfolios rather conservatively, the portfolios would consist primarily of bonds and mortgages with some equity and some private real estate.

When interest rates were higher, it wasn't uncommon for policies to pay 8 to 9 percent per year in annual interest payments and dividends. However, traditional life insurance policies are very sensitive to interest rates. In low-interest rate environments like the one that existed when this book was written in 2021, the policies tend to pay less interest to their policy owners than during periods of high interest rates. When the stock market was roaring in the 1990s, insurance companies started offering variable life insurance policies, which grew or declined based on the performance of underlying professionally managed sub-accounts. However, after the poor performance of the stock market in the 2000s, these products lost much of their appeal.

Over the last decade, Fixed Index Universal Life has increased in popularity. These contracts allow the owner to earn interest each year that is tied to the performance of an external market index, subject to a cap, spread, or participation rate—without the risk of loss in the years that the markets are down.

Many people subscribe to the mantra, "Buy term and invest the difference." However, this strategy has several flaws. People who promote that concept may be ignoring the impact of taxes and trading costs and assume that no advisory fees are being paid. This is highly unrealistic. Most importantly, they often incorrectly assume that the average investor will make the full returns of the stock market. Studies have shown that this just isn't the case. According to a prominent study by Dalbar, a Boston consulting firm, the average retail mutual fund investor substantially underperforms the S&P 500 depending on the time

---

https://longtermcare.acl.gov/the-basics/how-much-care-will-you-need.html

period by 5 to 7 percent per year.[12] This is partly because of the aforementioned high costs of investing, but also because investors tend to make investment decisions based on flawed logic and unfettered emotions. It's very difficult to remain a disciplined investor. Therefore, I submit that any vehicle that works on autopilot and doesn't have investment risk, and won't invite investors to make poor timing decisions that lead to underperformance, can be very beneficial.

I designed for myself my first cash value life insurance policy in 1997. Back then I only contributed $300 per month, but it still increased in value every year regardless of what the stock market did. There were times over the years when I needed money and I took funds out tax-free. I subsequently put them back when cash flow improved. Now I have over $170,000 in the contract, all from starting out with $300 per month. That's the power of tax-free compounding. I no longer contribute, but it continues to go up every year. However, I put six figures away in Index Universal Life contracts that I subsequently acquired. I also have four kids. The year they were born, I started a policy for each of them and I contribute $3,000 per year. The level of potentially tax-free income my kids are projected to have when they are at retirement age is impressive.

"I don't need insurance." This is an interesting thought. Anyone who says this simply means that either there is no economic loss at their death because they no longer make income from working or that they already have enough assets to provide for their family if they were to die. However, under that logic, there may be many assets that you don't need. You may not "need" a second or third home. Your family may not need 100 percent of your bank accounts or business accounts to maintain their desired lifestyle. However, very few people complain that their family's net worth is continuing to grow beyond what is needed. If you are in the fortunate position that you have a surplus of assets to maintain your desired lifestyle, then you are essentially managing that surplus of assets

---

[12] Dana Anspach. The Balance. August 28, 2020. "Why Average Investors Earn Below Average Market Returns." https://www.thebalance.com/why-average-investors-earn-below-average-market-returns-2388519; Wayne Duggan. MarketWatch. December 11, 2019. "Why Investing As An Individual Is So Difficult." https://www.marketwatch.com/story/why-investing-as-an-individual-is-so-difficult-2019-12-11

for your heirs. For most people we work with, their heirs are typically their children and grandchildren. Many people invest those funds in the stock market or the bond market. Others are more conservative and keep a lot of their money in savings. Some people invest in real estate.

The objective of these "investments" is usually to maximize the size of their children's inheritance. But what if there was a way to substantially grow your assets on a tax-free basis by the time you died? Would that be something you would consider, or could you do better in the stock market? As of 2021, the Dow Jones Industrial Average was trading at over 30,000. For your diversified stock/mutual fund to quadruple, the major indexes would likely have to quadruple. Will you live long enough to see the Dow Jones break 120,000? Maybe or maybe not. Will your money market account or bonds quadruple in your lifetime? Not likely.

If there was a way that you could multiply, perhaps even quadruple your assets tax-free by the time you died, that would be something to consider. The strategy that I'm talking about is single premium life insurance designed for the maximum death benefit. I routinely design life insurance policies that would provide a sizeable tax-free death benefit to the beneficiaries for people in their sixties[13]. The older you are, the less the leverage is but the sooner the tax-free payoff is anticipated. The internal rate of return upon death can be very attractive compared to other alternatives that don't have investment risk. Best of all, the government doesn't want one cent of the proceeds. All death benefit proceeds to a properly named beneficiary are 100 percent income tax free. Although your family may not need all that additional inheritance, they certainly won't be complaining about getting a larger inheritance than they had expected.

---

[13] Life insurance involves fees and expenses, including in some cases surrender penalties for early withdrawal. You often must qualify for it medically and financially.

CHAPTER ELEVEN

Sequence of Returns

All financial plans require a certain set of assumptions: How much income will one need in retirement? What is the expected rate of inflation? What are the expected returns of one's investment portfolio both before and during retirement? How long are you expected to live? Unfortunately, there is no way to predict any of these assumptions with absolute certainty. Therefore, in order to have a high probability of success, a plan must utilize conservative assumptions. What if inflation is higher than expected? What if you live to 105? What if your equity investments only return 6 percent instead of 7.13 percent? That last number represents historical returns of the S&P 500 for the 20-year period that ended in 2018.[14] One must also plan for various contingencies like the need for increased healthcare or a major financial recession.

Assuming an expected investment return can be very challenging, especially during retirement. One must assume both a gross return and a net return after fees and taxes, while accounting for additional uncertainty known as sequence of returns. Over any given period, the stock market will have a specific return. Some decades are better than others. From a mathematical standpoint, it is irrelevant if a given return over a specific time period is derived from better returns in the early part of the term or better returns in the latter part of the term. For instance, if year one is up 20 percent and year two is down 10 percent, the total two-year return is up 8 percent. Alternatively, if year one is down 10 percent and year two is up 20 percent, the total two-year return is plus 8 percent. However, this mathematical equivalency only applies if no additions or withdrawals are made to the investment over the term. For instance, for

---

[14] J.B. Maverick. Investopedia. February 19, 2020. "What is the Average Annual Return for the S&P 500?" https://www.investopedia.com/ask/answers/042415/what-average-annual-return-sp-500.asp

those saving for retirement and contributing periodically to their investment accounts, it's preferable that any negative years occur earlier while money is being added. Here's why: If the price of underlying investments fall, additional contributions will purchase additional shares at a lower price. On the other hand, if the early years are the better years, the periodic additional investments will purchase shares at a higher price, only to see the investment value fall during the subsequent "down" years. In this scenario, the investor is "Buying High."

When one finally enters retirement and is required to take withdrawals to create retirement income, the effects of sequence of returns can be dramatic. If your retirement starts off with a few bad years and you are taking income from your investments, your chances of running out of money increase significantly even if the market rebounds. For example, if you had $1,000,000 and you assumed a 6 percent return, you might think that you could spend 6 percent of the account value each year without touching the principal. This would be true if the portfolio earned a straight 6 percent without any variance. The chart below shows that a straight 6 percent return allows one to spend 6 percent per year ($60,000) without touching the principal. (These examples are hypothetical and do not represent any specific product or investment. For simplicity's sake, we have not deducted taxes or investment fees, which would reduce the figures shown here).

	Hypothetical return	Beginning Account Balance	Annual withdrawal
2001	6%	$1,000,000	-$60,000
2002	6%	$1,000,000	-$60,000
2003	6%	$1,000,000	-$60,000
2004	6%	$1,000,000	-$60,000
2005	6%	$1,000,000	-$60,000
2006	6%	$1,000,000	-$60,000
2007	6%	$1,000,000	-$60,000
2008	6%	$1,000,000	-$60,000
2009	6%	$1,000,000	-$60,000
2010	6%	$1,000,000	-$60,000
2011	6%	$1,000,000	-$60,000
2012	6%	$1,000,000	-$60,000
2013	6%	$1,000,000	-$60,000
2014	6%	$1,000,000	-$60,000
2015	6%	$1,000,000	-$60,000
2016	6%	$1,000,000	-$60,000
2017	6%	$1,000,000	-$60,000
2018	6%	$1,000,000	-$60,000
2019	6%	$1,000,000	-$60,000
2020	6%	$1,000,000	-$60,000
2021	6%	$1,000,000	
	6%		

	S&P 500 returns	Beginning Account Balance	Annual withdrawal
2001	-13.04%	$1,000,000	-$60,000
2002	-23.37%	$817,424	-$60,000
2003	26.38%	$580,414	-$60,000
2004	8.99%	$657,699	-$60,000
2005	3.00%	$651,432	-$60,000
2006	13.62%	$609,175	-$60,000
2007	3.53%	$623,973	-$60,000
2008	-38.49%	$583,881	-$60,000
2009	23.45%	$322,239	-$60,000
2010	12.78%	$323,735	-$60,000
2011	0.00%	$297,440	-$60,000
2012	13.41%	$237,440	-$60,000
2013	29.60%	$201,234	-$60,000
2014	11.39%	$183,040	-$60,000
2015	-0.73%	$137,054	-$60,000
2016	9.54%	$76,492	-$60,000
2017	19.42%	$18,065	-$60,000
2018	-6.24%	-$50,079	-$60,000
2019	28.88%	-$103,210	-$60,000
2020	16.26%	-$210345	-$60,000
2021		-$314,303	

But life doesn't move in a straight line, and neither does the market. Financial planning would be much easier if it was simple to find instruments that provided 6 percent yearly interest without risk or volatility. Volatility is the price investors must pay to potentially achieve greater returns. As you can see from the chart, the S&P 500 averaged 7.07 percent from 2000 to 2020 before fees and taxes and investor underperformance from poor market timing decisions. One might assume that an investor who had an investment that performed similarly to the S&P 500 and earned 7.07 percent per year over a twenty-year time period could easily withdraw 6 percent per year of the initial investment without touching the principal.

Yet if one started with one million in 1999 and withdrew $60,000 per year, their one million would have been depleted in fewer than twenty years. As you can see, the portfolio that earned 6 percent per year held up better than the portfolio that averaged 7.07 percent per year for two reasons: one, the sequence of returns was not favorable. In this case, there were several "down" years early. When money was distributed for income, part of the investment account had to be sold at a low point to provide that income. Once the funds are distributed, when the invariable rebound occurs, there is less money participating in the rebound. The investor is essentially selling at a low and locking in losses. Two, the portfolio with a consistent return of 6 percent offers much lower volatility. Lower returns can be just fine if they mean you also don't have wide variations to overcome from extreme highs and lows.

Now, to be clear, I am not suggesting that there is an actual investment, which incurs risk and volatility, that is available to provide the consistency reflected in the chart with uniform 6 percent returns. But the mathematics here are what's important: clearly, consistent positive performance offers something in a portfolio that one won't find in the ups and downs of typical market performance. The question becomes this: How can one design a portfolio that has less volatility and therefore, less sequence of returns risk, especially during the retirement income phase? The classic way to help reduce volatility is through diversification,[15] which entails ownership in many types of investments. For example, the equity part of a portfolio could have large, medium, small, international, and developing markets. This kind of diversification has become less effective, though, since we are part of a global economy more than ever before. In most years, these equity asset classes have become more highly correlated. One alternative is certain "smart beta" investments that can be constructed utilizing only stocks with less volatility. These stocks tend to go down less during market downturns.

Historically, treasury bonds have been used to reduce volatility in one's portfolio. Bonds have typically rallied during times of market downturns as investors flee to safety. The problem with bonds is that they not only offer a minimal reward, but they have a decent amount of interest rate risk. Bonds lose value if interest rates rise and gain value if interest rates fall. Most people think that there is very little room for interest rates to go any lower.

Another way to further diversify your portfolio is to use alternative investments that aren't publicly traded. These investments are typically comprised of private real estate, private loans, and private equity. They often have investment and other unique risks, but they also may involve less market risk. In other words, the value of these investments tends to fluctuate less than traditional stock and bond investments. Additionally, there are certain products that can't lose principal and therefore have much lower volatility. In any case, regardless of which investments or products you chose, retirees should generally have a portion of their assets invested conservatively so that in the years the more aggressive portion of the portfolio is down, there is a safe place to take the retirement income that may be necessary for the given period.

For example, take a look at the chart below, which shows how market volatility can affect your portfolio's overall bottom line. Note that while the average rate of return of the S&P 500 index over this time period is higher than the 6 percent fixed investment, the portfolio mirroring the S&P 500 index has dropped by almost 100 percent in value while the fixed portfolio remains intact. This reinforces the dramatic impact of the sequence of returns during the distribution phase of your lifetime, and how you can run out of money quickly if you have not addressed this crucial risk.

---

[15] Neither diversification nor asset allocation can ensure a profit or guarantee against losses in a declining market.

		S&P		6% Fixed Investment	
Year	Yearly Income	Amount Left	Return	Amount Left	Return
2001	$60,000	$1,000,000	-13.04	$1,000,000	6.00%
2002	$60,000	$817,424	-23.37	$1,000,000	6.00%
2003	$60,000	$580,414	26.38	$1,000,000	6.00%
2004	$60,000	$657,699	8.99	$1,000,000	6.00%
2005	$60,000	$651,432	3.00	$1,000,000	6.00%
2006	$60,000	$609,175	13.62	$1,000,000	6.00%
2007	$60,000	$623,973	3.53	$1,000,000	6.00%
2008	$60,000	$583,881	-38.49	$1,000,000	6.00%
2009	$60,000	$322,239	23.45	$1,000,000	6.00%
2010	$60,000	$323,735	12.78	$1,000,000	6.00%
2011	$60,000	$297,440	0.00	$1,000,000	6.00%
2012	$60,000	$237,440	13.41	$1,000,000	6.00%
2013	$60,000	$201,234	29.60	$1,000,000	6.00%
2014	$60,000	$183,040	11.39	$1,000,000	6.00%
2015	$60,000	$137,054	-0.73	$1,000,000	6.00%
2016	$60,000	$76,492	9.54	$1,000,000	6.00%
2017	$60,000	$18,065	19.42	$1,000,000	6.00%
2018	$60,000	-$50,079	-6.24	$1,000,000	6.00%
2019	$60,000	-$103,210	28.88	$1,000,000	6.00%
2020	$60,000	-$210,345	16.26	$1,000,000	6.00%
2021	$60,000	-$314,303		$1,000,000	6.00%
		Average Return	6.92%	Average Return	6.00%

CHAPTER TWELVE

Alternative Investments

As the name implies, alternative investments are assets other than traditional stocks, bonds, or cash (or funds comprised of traditional stocks and bonds). Any other asset that can appreciate or generate income could be considered an alternative investment.

For example, purchasing an office building or a collectible piece of art could be classified as an alternative investment. Many investors have been underwhelmed by the results of their stock investments and bond buyers have been watching yields drop over the last decade. Meanwhile, even stock investors who have enjoyed great returns on stocks since the last crash of 2008 are less optimistic about the near-term prospects of traditional stock investments. After a twelve-year bull market where the S&P 500 averaged more than 13 percent per year up to December 31, 2020, stocks were trading at historically high valuations.[16] Bonds were offering very low yields compared to prior decades, and the Federal Reserve recently lowered rates even further. For better or worse, stocks —including ETFs and mutual funds—remain the assets that comprise the vast majority of retail investors' portfolios.

Unlike the typical investor, the wealthiest investors, institutions, and endowment funds generally invest entirely differently by utilizing nontraditional investments. Traditionally, if you had enough capital, you had access to investments that most retail investors couldn't access. Large institutions and wealthy families tend to have significant exposure to alternative investments like private equity (ownership interest in smaller companies that are not publicly traded), private debt (loans to smaller non-public companies), private real estate, hedge funds, currencies, and commodities.

---

[16] Thomas Franck. CNBC. March 14, 2020. "A Look at Bear and Bull Markets Through History." https://www.cnbc.com/2020/03/14/a-look-at-bear-and-bull-markets-through-history.html

According to the Yale University website, the university manages almost $30 billion in its endowment fund, yet allocates only about 10 percent of its assets to traditional domestic marketable securities.[17] Why would that be? Yale's endowment fund obviously can afford to hire very smart advisors. Their team of advisors has one job: to put Yale's endowment fund in the best possible risk-adjusted investments. They must be doing something right as Yale's endowment fund has averaged 12.6 percent per year for thirty years. That return is significantly higher than a traditional portfolio of stocks and bonds. Perhaps retail advisors should consider the strategies of Yale's endowment fund.[18]

Many of these alternative investments have historically outperformed traditional stocks and bonds. Private equity has the potential for higher returns than publicly traded stocks and private debt typically might offer higher yields than publicly traded corporate bonds.[19] Granted, you can't rely on past performance to predict what any investment or asset class will do in the future. Bear this in mind: Alternative investments typically have longer holding periods and require higher minimum investments. They are sometimes not regulated by the SEC, which could necessitate a deeper level of due diligence by investors or their advisors. They are also typically not as liquid as traditional investments. However, with less liquidity often comes less volatility. Therefore, lack of liquidity is not necessarily a detriment for long-term investors.

Over the past several years, large financial institutions have created alternative investments that are accessible by retail investors for much lower minimum investments and enhanced liquidity features, which could afford investors access to their money in as little as one year. Advising clients about which alternative investments to allocate to is an area where financial advisors can provide value to their clients. Because there are so many alternative investment products available today to the retail investor, it can be difficult to evaluate them all and determine which opportunities have the potential for the best risk-adjusted expected

---

[17] Yale News. September 27, 2019. "Investment Return of 5.7% Brings Yale Endowment Value to $30.3 Billion." https://news.yale.edu/2019/09/27/investment-return-57-brings-yale-endowment-value-303-billion

[18] Yale Investments Office. "The Yale Investments Office." http://investments.yale.edu/.

[19] Tyler Gallagher. *Forbes*. January 31, 2020. "How Alternative Investing Can Improve Your Portfolio." https://www.forbes.com/sites/theyec/2020/01/31/how-alternative-investing-can-improve-your-portfolio/#1ddb153c54aa

returns. Advisory firms that offer these strategies should perform that due diligence for their clients.

Although these alternative investments have historically only been accessible by the large institutions and ultra-wealthy, they have become increasingly more available to the typical accredited investor.

To be an accredited investor, you would need a current income (greater than $200,000 per year for an individual or $300,000 for a married couple). Alternatively, you would be an accredited investor if your family net worth, excluding your residence, exceeds one million. Since this number includes current savings and investments—among them retirement accounts—there is a surprisingly large number of qualified households in the United States. Verify Investor data estimates that at the end of 2018, more than 10 million, or about 8 percent of households in the U.S., would qualify as accredited—and that was before the SEC ruling that also expanded the definition of accredited investors to include employees of various investing companies as well as independent financial advisors.[20] Despite their increased accessibility, relatively few accredited investors are taking advantage of alternatives in their portfolios.

Part of the reason the public isn't as aware of these investments is that there are strict rules about advertising these investments. These investments are typically not permitted to be advertised to the general public. Retail advisors probably need to do a better job of educating themselves about available alternatives and then include them in the portfolios they manage, where it's suitable. The alternative investments take many different forms, such as pools of loans to well-established and highly profitable businesses secured by corporate assets. Other options include equity in non-public companies with strong venture capital backing and many different forms of real estate, from the development of new projects to the operation of broad portfolios of rental properties. Many have attractive liquidity features, and are often tax-advantaged, when held in taxable accounts. The investments can be held in existing investment account and retirement accounts, so many times, it's not even necessary for an investor to open any new accounts.

A very attractive feature of most alternative investments is that their

---

[20] VerifyInvestor.com. October 8, 2018. "How Many Accredited Investors Are In the U.S.? https://blog.verifyinvestor.com/blog/2018/10/8/how-many-accredited-investors-are-in-the-us; U.S. Securities and Exchange Commission. August 26, 2020. "SEC Modernizes the Accredited Investor Definition." https://www.sec.gov/news/press-release/2020-191

value is often determined based upon the intrinsic, tangible value of the assets in the investments, and not by the emotions of the general public, which drive the value of the stock market. The assets generally span a large group of individual investments, providing a level of diversification. Because the values tend to be more stable during economic downturns, it can help protect the investor from emotionally cashing out during market downturns, which is one of the greatest reasons that most individual investors greatly underperform the overall market.

An increasingly common alternative investment is commodities. They have become more of a mainstream investment since the turn of the century. Commodities don't pay dividends, but they also don't go out of business. They can provide stability in turbulent market periods.

Be careful to know the difference between speculating in commodities and investing in them, however. Opening a commodities account and trading in futures contracts—a key plot point in the movie "Trading Places," in fact—isn't really investing; it's speculating. Investing in managed futures funds allows you to potentially catch large moves in the commodities market, whether those moves trend up or down.

Private mortgages, which are loans that are secured by real estate, can be used to create relatively high levels of income. Potential default risk can be mitigated through proper underwriting of the loan and the use of low debt to loan ratios.

Additionally, banks can create a wide variety of structured notes that can be designed to create growth or income. I will be discussing these vehicles in more detail in a subsequent chapter.

CHAPTER THIRTEEN

Fixed Indexed Annuities

The public's interest in participating in any investment is directly correlated to its recent performance. When real estate is steadily rising, people want to buy real estate. When gold has periods of large increases in price, investors want more gold, and when stocks are doing well, people feel like stocks are a great investment. At the time I had entered the financial services industry in 1996, stocks had been on a roll. People viewed stocks as the preferred method of growing their wealth. They weren't overly concerned about downside protection.

That all changed in the 2000s, starting with the tech crash and then culminating in 2008. When the United States faced its worst financial crisis since the Great Depression, stock investments were decimated. Major financial institutions failed or were bailed out by the government. People were even scared to put their money in the bank, let alone into riskier investments like stocks. They were, for the first time in my career, very concerned about the safety of their investments. It was during this period of stock market carnage that I attended a conference with a life insurance company that was introducing a new product: a fixed index annuity. The contract would give contract holders interest equal to 90 percent of the returns of the S&P 500, minus a 1.5 percent charge per year with no risk to their principal, without ever being invested in the market. Moreover, every four years, any interest credited would get locked in and protected from subsequent stock market corrections.

I was skeptical. How could you earn interest tied to the stock index to make 90 percent of upside without market risk and then lock in that interest? The actuary explained that the company would put a percentage of the premiums collected into their portfolio of bonds to ensure the insurance company would have enough money to return the investor's principal or make income payments to them, as well as generate a profit for the company. With the excess funds, the company would buy option contracts on, say, the S&P Index 500, which becomes more valuable if the index goes up. This allows the insurance company to pay you interest when the S&P 500 goes up. When I returned from the conference, I quickly called my clients, who were paralyzed with the fear of the current economic meltdown and presented a conservative alternative. For those clients for whom it made sense, they acquired their first fixed index annuity in late 2008 and early 2009. The product allowed my clients to receive the potential for interest tied to the index each annuity year, with no investment risk. The primary risk was the credit risk of the issuing insurance company, which backs all their contractual guarantees. This turned out to be a solid vehicle at the time for those who were too scared to invest in the stock market, even though, in retrospect, it might have been one of the absolute best times to invest in stocks as the market was just about hitting bottom.

The concept of earning interest when the market is going up but not losing when it's going down, while locking in your interest, can be very appealing. However, not all annuities are created equally. Unfortunately, not all advisors and insurance agents have a thorough understanding of how these products work. Moreover, the average consumer is not always able to understand all the significant nuances. The wide disparity of fixed index annuity performance and potentially poor recommendations by many advisors is one of the reasons that there are so many mixed opinions about these products. The best index annuities offer the potential for attractive interest rates along with the opportunity for guaranteed lifetime income, while the worst can leave the consumer with unfulfilled expectations. Therefore, I think it is important to be able to understand what to look for in a fixed index annuity in order to achieve optimal results.

As I previously indicated, there are certain techniques insurance companies use to entice consumers to purchase their products. One of the things to look out for is complicated crediting methods. One method is called a monthly sum. Each year, the issuing company adds up the index increases for each month throughout the previous year. You can receive an interest credit for this, adjusted by a cap, spread, or participation rate. For example, if you have a 2 percent monthly cap, you might think to yourself (or your agent might lead you to believe) that you could make 2 percent per month or 24 percent per year (assuming a 2 percent monthly cap) in a good year. While that may be theoretically true, it's highly unrealistic. Each month, your account can make up to 2 percent. But at the end of twelve months, the company will add up all the up months capped at 2 percent and subtract all the down months (uncapped) to come up with the total yearly interest. One bad month, down 10 percent, for example, even if followed by a month of plus 10 percent (capped at 2 percent) results in negative 8 percent for the two-month period. In other words, one bad month can ruin the whole year with this method.

Historically, most up years have at least one really bad month. Occasionally this method can produce a good year. Often, however, this method can also leave consumers disappointed. Another potential crediting method is called the monthly average method. Each month the closing price of the index is calculated, and the twelve-monthly prices are averaged together and compared to the initial price. In a year where the index rises 10 percent, the monthly average method could result in interest of only 3-4 percent—especially if more of the index gains occurred at the end of the year. The easiest crediting method to track is called point to point. Whatever the index makes from one annuity contract anniversary to the next, you will receive interest subject to a cap (limit), spread, or participation rate. The first fixed index annuities I recommended to clients were point to point with 90 percent participation and a four-year reset. This means that every four years, any interest credited would get locked in. Conversely, if the index was down, the index resets and starts over at the low point to the benefit of the contract owner. Today, most fixed index annuities available reset every year or every two years, which is much better than a four-year reset. The shorter the reset period, the more frequently any credited interest gets locked in, or losing years are erased with a new low starting point. As we started approaching the tenth year of the most recent bull market and many analysts warned of an inevitable recession, I started utilizing fixed index annuities with annual resets.

Many consumers are attracted to fixed index annuities because they are enticed by the prospect of receiving a large "upfront" bonus. If you think that insurance companies offer bonuses to be altruistic, you'll be disappointed. Think twice before making an investment decision based on a large bonus, which is simply front-loaded interest. Annuity companies sometimes attract consumers by either offering competitive interest rate opportunities or the appearance of them. Although annuity owners love seeing an immediate increase in their account values from a bonus when investing, the owner could forfeit the bonus upon early termination of the contract unless they pass away before the term of the contract ends. In other instances, the consumer realizes the bonus only if they take income from the contract in a specific manner. Bonus annuities also often have lower caps and participation rates, higher spreads, and longer surrender charge periods. Therefore, the bonus is simply part of the interest that the annuity owner will earn over the term of the contract and is certainly not free money. We all know that insurance companies aren't in business to give away free money. So why do they give them? In my opinion, there are two primary reasons insurance companies offer bonuses:

1. As a strategy to actually pay LESS interest without decreasing sales. Without a bonus, the insurance company will need to offer more competitive interest rates to attract customers. With a bonus, customers will be less likely to scrutinize the interest crediting method.
2. To entice consumers to exchange their existing annuity contracts. Many unethical agents attempting to make more commissions promote the bonus to "offset" a surrender charge when switching annuities. A bonus is just some of the interest that will be paid over the term of the contract and does not "offset" the surrender charge incurred from switching annuities. It has been my experience that annuity contracts offering bonuses will usually underperform similar annuities without bonuses. Consumers should choose contracts paying the most interest over the term of the annuity contract and avoid being seduced by illusory bonuses when evaluating a potential annuity investment.

Finally, many companies make a lot of money selling income riders on their fixed index annuities. On the positive side, income riders do guarantee the contract owner a lifetime income stream with some potential extra benefits in the event one needs long-term care. That can certainly provide financial comfort.

Now the bad news: Some fixed index annuity income riders can be illusory and misleading. In most cases, the guaranteed income that the rider provides is calculated based on a fictitious income account value that is used in most cases solely for the calculation of lifetime income. This "income account value" has no real value. You can't access it or cash it out. It typically starts with a value equal to your initial premium, plus any bonus. It usually increases each year by a fixed percentage of 6 to 8 percent. When the contract owner is ready to start taking income, they are permitted to draw a pre-determined percentage of that income rider value (typically 5 to 6 percent) from their ACCOUNT VALUE. What this means is that at a certain point you can withdraw a fixed amount from your account each year without running out of income even if you deplete the account. Since fixed index annuities cannot lose any money due to investment risk, you generally need to live a long time before getting any value from your income rider. From what I have seen, not all annuity holders live long enough to actually receive a financial benefit from their income riders; with a few exceptions, income riders have no residual value at death.

One problem I have is that life insurance agents continually allow their prospective clients to believe that a 6 to 8 percent roll-up on the income value riders is their return. That is simply not true. The return on an annuity is based only on the account value. The income rider value annual increase is completely unrelated to the account value.

Typically, there is an annual charge for the income rider. This charge, which is usually a little less than 1 percent per year, is based on the income rider value, which is always higher than the account value. As an example, you put $100,000 into an annuity with an optional income rider, and after ten years, the account value has grown to $130,000, and the income rider value has grown to $170,000. The annual fee for the income rider at .90 is $1,530 per year. This fee is deducted from the account value each year along with the income withdrawals. Even when the account value is approaching zero, the annual fee is still $1,530 per year. As a result, income riders make it more likely to reduce the inheritance left to one's heirs. Because I believe that income riders tend to be oversold, I meet many people who have purchased income riders, yet have no need to access the income, have never started taking income, nor do they ever plan to. In such circumstances, an income rider is not suitable.

One final point on this topic: In general, fixed index annuities offering income riders tend to pay less interest on the account values than index annuities that do not have income riders. There are two reasons why this typically happens. People who buy income riders and agents who sell them are more focused on guaranteed income than account growth. As a result, insurance companies competing in that space don't need to offer the most attractive interest crediting methods. The second reason is the income rider annual fee, which can be a drag on the performance. For these reasons, I tend to recommend fixed index annuities that do not offer a bonus or an income rider but have the most attractive crediting methods and, therefore, provide what I believe are better growth opportunities.

CHAPTER FOURTEEN

Protecting Against Elder Abuse

"**M**om, I need to add my name to your accounts so I can help you manage your finances and pay your bills."

This is what my aunt said to my grandmother, who was living in a nursing home. Many people who were previously self-sufficient and highly independent become dependent on others once their health starts to diminish as they age. Unfortunately, this is the exact time in their lives that they become easy targets for elder abuse. Sadly, my grandmother was victimized by her daughter, who transferred all her mother's assets into her own accounts. Even though my grandmother's last will and testament directed that everything would be distributed equally to her two daughters, by the time she died there were no assets left to distribute.

Perhaps my aunt believed that she was "entitled" to the money because she was the only local relative that was occasionally visiting. Perhaps my aunt even got verbal authorization from my grandmother to make financial decisions. Or maybe she just stole the money because no one was in the position to stop her. In any case, an elderly person was taken advantage of.

According to a global study, more than 15 percent of adults over the age of sixty are victims of elder abuse.[21] Elder abuse can occur in many forms: physical, emotional, and even financial. In truth, this figure is likely conservative at best because many instances of abuse are never reported. How many times has a child orchestrated lifetime gifts to the detriment of their siblings? How frequently is an attorney brought in at

---

[21] Yonjie Yon, Christopher Mikton, Zachary Gassoumis, Kathleen Wilber. Lancet Global Health. February 5, 2017. "Elder Abuse Prevalence in Community Settings." https://pubmed.ncbi.nlm.nih.gov/28104184/

the eleventh hour to change estate planning documents to favor one heir over another? These types of things happen all the time and often are never reported.

I recently had a client that was left a substantial sum in a relative's will. Unfortunately, while the relative was 88 years old and lying in a hospital bed, another relative brought an attorney into the hospital and convinced the octogenarian to change her will and exclude my client. My client's relative died a few months later. She and some other disinherited beneficiaries teamed up to file a lawsuit and recover the originally intended inheritance. With my assistance, we were able to reach an acceptable settlement with the new beneficiary, but my client got much less than she was supposed to in the original will. This is one example of a common case of elder abuse that rarely gets reported.

At some point in the life cycle, many people develop diminished memory and judgment. They also experience a reduction in physical and mental capacity. When this occurs, seniors often need to rely on family members or even outside caregivers for help with daily activities of living. Sadly, statistics show elder abuse comes at the hands of family members 60 percent of the time.[22] Most people can't even fathom being in a position where they need to rely on family members or caregivers just to survive. However, once one becomes dependent on others for basic needs, they lose their autonomy and even the ability to make decisions without relying on their primary caregivers.

As an estate planning attorney and a financial advisor, I have seen many instances of both emotional and financial abuse. Adult children who become caregivers often may feel entitled to "compensation" in the form of loans or gifts. It can be very traumatic when a family member who you trust and potentially rely on violates that trust to gain a financial benefit. A child that orchestrates the transfer to themselves of a disproportionate share of parental assets can destroy family

---

[22] J. Peterson, D. Burnes, P. Caccamise, A. Mason, C. Henderson, M. Wells, and M. Lachs. *Journal of General Internal Medicine*. 2014. "Financial exploitation of older adults: a population-based prevalence study." 29(12), 1615–23. doi: 10.1007/s11606-014-2946-2

relationships. I am sure my grandparents never wanted their legacy to be one of lawsuits and broken relationships between their children.

Senior adults should implement some safeguards to protect themselves and their families. One should proceed cautiously before giving a relative signatory authority on one's accounts. One way to guard against potential abuse is to create a system of checks and balances. If it is necessary to grant a power of attorney, consider granting a joint power of attorney, which will require two agents to sign off on any transaction. The use of an attorney or a CPA as a co-agent can add an extra layer of protection. Another option is allowing multiple family members to receive duplicate account statements so they can monitor your accounts for any suspicious activity.

I once created a durable power of attorney for a very sick client. I met with her and one of her daughters to allow her daughters to effectuate transactions in her accounts. However, shortly after granting her daughter a power of attorney, the daughter requested a $10,000 transfer from the mother's account to "pay for medical bills" for the mother. A couple of weeks later, she made another request for $10,000. I asked the daughter if she minded if we did a conference call with her only sister and eventual co-heir to the mother's estate to make sure that both daughters were aware of the transfer request. Luckily, the other daughter had been in the loop, and the funds were indeed needed for medical expenses. In this case, there was no elder abuse. However, I will always be vigilant to help ensure that none of my clients are getting victimized on my watch.

It's very hard for many successful, independent people to ever envision a scenario in which they lack the mental or physical capacity to prevent others from taking advantage of them. But the numbers don't lie: It's happening more and more frequently. Luckily, there are steps that can be taken to ensure protection:

1. Draft a revocable trust with successor co-trustees that can manage your assets if you become incapacitated.

2. Execute a durable power of attorney with two or more trusted family members or professionals that can act on your behalf

3. Request duplicate investment statements going to trusted family members

4. Make sure your children and your advisors know each other

5. Have a trusted friend advisor or family member that is impartial and can be called upon to be one's advocate in the event of a potentially abusive situation

CHAPTER FIFTEEN

So Taxing

The United States has an interesting history with taxation. There was no federal income tax in America until 1913. That year, the Sixteenth Amendment was ratified to the Constitution, thus granting Congress the power to collect taxes on personal income.

Similarly, there was no state sales tax in any state until 1921.[23] From a federal standpoint, Congress makes tax laws to create revenue to run the country. There seems to be a continuous debate about optimal tax rates. How much money does the government need? What is the current deficit? Should the wealthy pay a disproportionate share? What is the best tax program for supporting economic growth? These are all policy questions that are the subject of constant debate.

One of the biggest arguments by proponents for lower taxes is that if taxes are too high, overall revenue can get smaller. In the 1980s, economist Arthur Laffer published a theory known as the Laffer Curve to show the relationship between tax rates and the amount of tax revenue collected by governments. Laffer argued that sometimes cutting tax rates can increase total tax revenue because if taxes get too high, taxed activities, such as work and investment, will be discouraged. The Laffer Curve was used as a basis for tax cuts in the 1980s with apparent success. Until the early 1980s, the top tax rates were as high as 70 percent. The Economic Recovery Tax Act of 1981 slashed the highest rate from 70 to 50 percent and indexed the brackets for inflation. Then, the Tax Reform Act of 1986 expanded the tax base and dropped the top rate to 28 percent for tax years beginning in 1988. Lawmakers claimed that they would never have to raise the 28 percent top rate. Yet the promise of a 28 percent

---

[23] Amy Fontinelle. Investopedia. Dec. 31, 2020. "A Brief History of Taxes in the U.S." https://www.investopedia.com/articles/tax/10/history-taxes.asp

top rate lasted three years before it was broken. During the 1990s, the top rate jumped to 39.6 percent.

The Economic Growth and Tax Relief and Reconciliation Act of 2001 dropped the highest income tax rate to 35 percent from 2003 to 2010. The Tax Relief, Unemployment Insurance Reauthorization, and Job Creation Act of 2010 maintained the 35 percent tax rate through 2012. The American Taxpayer Relief Act of 2012 increased the highest income tax rate to 39.6 percent. The Patient Protection and Affordable Care Act added 3.8 percent, making the maximum federal income tax rate 43.4 percent. The highest income tax rate was lowered to 37 percent for tax years beginning in 2018. However, the additional 3.8 percent is still applicable, making the maximum federal income tax rate 40.8 percent at the time I authored this book.

Although tax policy is largely used to maximize government revenue, it's also used to encourage or discourage certain behavior. People get favorable tax treatment for having children, being married, saving for retirement, owning life insurance, owning a fuel-efficient car, investing in a business or real estate, and contributing to charity. Similarly, people frequently pay extra taxes on the purchase of cigarettes and alcohol, or if they don't own health insurance.

Figuring out how to navigate the current tax code to minimize one's tax liability, not only in the present year but in future years, can be challenging. One of the things the government has always encouraged is saving for retirement. There is a myriad of ways to contribute to a retirement account, from Roth IRAs to any number of employee-sponsored retirement plans. All except the Roth (which have funding rules resulting in relatively small contributions) allow for a current tax deduction and the ability to grow the retirement account on a tax-deferred basis. CPAs love current tax deductions and generally encourage their clients to take full advantage of them. For many people who are in or near retirement, their retirement accounts often make up a significant portion of their retirement assets. These are the exact assets in which the government has a keen interest. Not only is Uncle Sam waiting eagerly for retirees to make withdrawals from these accounts so that they may be taxed as ordinary income, but Congress also has passed laws that require retirees to take money out of their retirement accounts once they have reached age seventy-two.

The wild card in this whole transaction is that no one knows what taxes will be in any given year. Here is what we do know: as of 2020, taxes are relatively low compared to historical tax rates. Taxes are scheduled to go up in 2026. The government is facing a huge current deficit that is only expected to increase as baby boomers leave the workforce and start collecting Social Security. Retirees have two choices, continue to defer taking retirement income until they hit required minimum distributions or proactively withdraw IRA funds or systematically convert to Roth IRAs during the years, we are in a low tax bracket. Either way, retirees or their heirs will be paying taxes at some level on withdrawals from retirement accounts.

Each of us must determine how to dissolve our retirement account "partnership" with the IRS. What is the optimal strategy? There isn't necessarily a right or wrong answer because no one knows for sure what tax rates will be in the future. No one knows what political parties will be controlling Congress and the executive branch. However, we know this: married couples who make less than $100,000 before the standard deductions are only in the 12 percent tax bracket. If they make less than about $195,000, they're in the 22 percent tax bracket. Making withdrawals or doing partial Roth conversions are arguably very attractive from both a historical perspective and a forward-looking perspective. When considering how much of one's IRA should be withdrawn or converted to a Roth IRA each year, one needs to be able to estimate their current tax bracket and then calculate the cost for additional withdrawals if you need the money, or the cost of Roth conversions if you don't need the money. Let us assume that you are married filing jointly, and your adjusted gross income is $120,000. That puts you in the 22 percent marginal tax bracket. (It's only 12 percent up to $78,950.) That means you can convert up to $48,000 more at 22 percent tax rates and after that another approximate $150,000 at 24 percent. This is a concept called bracket stuffing. You might be thinking why should I pay extra taxes now instead of continuing to defer? For one, we already know that starting in 2026, $132,000 of adjusted gross income will put you in the 28 percent bracket if a future Congress does not enact additional increases. Moreover, if your beneficiaries are in a higher tax bracket or if they reside in a state with state income taxes, those retirement accounts will eventually be taxed at a bracket that could easily be over 50 percent once the tax brackets revert to their prior levels. In addition, 2020 tax laws enacted in the SECURE Act essentially eliminate the ability of one's children to "stretch" out IRA income over their lifetimes. Instead, the extension period has been shortened to ten years for most non-spousal beneficiaries. Therefore, there is a window of opportunity to dissolve your retirement account "partnership" with the IRS on very favorable terms.

Since we must consider the tax ramifications of making any investment, it's important to understand that the government also created tax laws that encourage real estate investments. When an investor invests in real estate, they must pay taxes on the income produced. However, those taxes are reduced by a concept called depreciation. For accounting purposes, you can "depreciate" the value of the building, which directly offsets the annual income tax liability. Even though the real estate is appreciating in market value from a tax standpoint, you are permitted to treat it like it's losing value. When you eventually sell the property, you will realize all that income but only as a "capital gain," which is taxed at much lower rates than ordinary income. Many successful people have taken advantage of this tax treatment and have become wealthy from real estate investments. According to Forbes, about 10 percent of the world's billionaires created their wealth from real estate. A significant portion of these investors were very "hands-on" over the years in the development and management of their properties.[24]

Real estate investors face a dilemma in turning their actively managed real estate investments into a passive retirement plan. Once they sell their real estate, they will owe federal and maybe state income taxes on all realized gains. Since most real estate investors have been depreciating their properties for tax purposes, there may be little or no tax basis

---

[24] Will Yakowicz. *Forbes.* March 9, 2020. "How the World's Billionaires Got So Rich." https://www.forbes.com/sites/willyakowicz/2019/03/09/how-the-worlds-billionaires-got-so-rich/#7b9264ac6ae6

remaining. Secondly, if they cash out and pay taxes, it may be difficult to earn as much income with their after-tax proceeds as they were earning prior to the sale.

Fortunately, the IRS currently allows real estate investors to exchange one property for another without paying taxes on the gains. There are certain procedures that must be followed. Specifically, the owner of the old property must be the same as the owner of the replacement property. Also, a qualified intermediary must hold the sales proceeds of the liquidated property to use for the purchase of the new property.

Not only do real estate investors get great tax treatment while owning and managing real estate, even when it's time to sell, but there will also continue to be very favorable tax strategies at their disposal. For investors looking to enjoy more leisure time, swapping an actively managed property for another actively managed property doesn't solve any problems. Therefore, the investor must find a property that can be managed passively. Several large real estate companies offer turnkey 1031 exchange diversified passive real estate investments, which could be attractive to investors looking for tax efficiency and predictable passive retirement income. Exchanged property will receive a full step up-in-tax basis upon the owner's death.

The tax-free exchange used to be available for artwork and collectibles; however, it is now only available for real estate. When one sells a stock for a profit, the euphoria of making a big profit will typically be tempered by the capital gains tax of up to 20 percent (as well as, potentially, state tax), which is due shortly thereafter.

However, there is now a way to delay and reduce those taxes with an investment in a Qualified Opportunity Zone Fund. The Tax Cuts and Jobs Act of 2017 creates a huge financial tax incentive for investments in low-income areas called Qualified Opportunity Zones. These low-income zones are in both inner cities and rural areas. Each state can designate areas to qualify as opportunity zones. These areas must be certified by the U.S. Secretary of the Treasury. An entity such as a corporation or a partnership may register as a Qualified Opportunity Fund provided that at least 90 percent of its assets are in designated opportunity zones.

If one invests all or part of their realized profits within 180 days following the sale in an Opportunity Fund, all capital gains from the sale will be deferred until the sale of the new investment or on Dec. 31, 2026, whichever comes first. Additionally, the investor will get a 10 percent increase in basis if the fund is held for at least five years.

Finally, if the investor holds the fund for ten years, they will pay no capital gains on the fund's increase in value. Additionally, unlike a 1031 exchange, which requires strict adherence to multiple formalities (such as the use of a qualified intermediary and like-to-like ownership transfer), the process of investing in an opportunity zone fund is relatively easy. Simply invest all or part of the profits within 180 days of the sale and taxes will be deferred. Although people are very excited that this law allows for the deferral and reduction of current capital gains, the fact that one can make a real estate investment and realize significant appreciation without having to pay any taxes on that appreciation is very powerful.

This is a unique opportunity to not only defer and reduce capital gains taxes but also an opportunity to help society by improving areas in most need of development.

The bottom line is that tax planning is an essential part of financial planning. While many tax professionals are focused almost exclusively on reducing the current year's tax liability, it's important to create and implement long-term tax strategies to maximize one's probability of success in retirement. Also, keep in mind that many of these tax savings strategies entail other unique risks (such as liquidity risk for real estate investments), so its advisable to work with a qualified tax, legal, and financial team to implement strategies for your unique circumstances.

CHAPTER SIXTEEN

Planning for Long-Term Care

"If you had an additional five million dollars, would you live any differently?"

I typically ask this question to most new prospective clients to uncover any bucket list items they would love to have or experience but feel are unattainable. A vast majority of people state that they would not live altogether differently, even if they possessed more wealth. By the time they have reached retirement, most people have established a lifestyle with which they are comfortable. It's a straightforward process to create a plan to meet predictable financial needs. However, two significant impediments to the success of an income plan that is otherwise well-constructed are longevity risk and unexpected expenses related to healthcare. Many people are simply not comfortable even thinking about those topics. I have had the following dialogue with several prospective clients.

Keith: "So tell me about what planning you have done to deal with the potential need for long-term care expenses."

Prospective client: "We really haven't done any long-term care planning. If I ever get in a position like that, I'm just gonna have them pull the plug."

Obviously, there is no plug to pull that ends one's life simply because they need assistance with the activities of daily living.

Unfortunately, this is simply how clients rationalize not planning for potential long-term care needs. They just try not to think about it.

The reality is that most people will need some long-term care. In fact, 69 percent of those turning sixty-five in 2020 will need long-term care during their lives, according to longtermcare.gov. That care will last an average of three years. People are living longer and longer. The increase in life expectancies equates to longer periods in which they will require care.[25]

According to a report by Genworth, the median annual cost of an assisted-living facility was recently more than $48,000, while it cost upward of $90,000 for a semi-private room at a nursing home.[26] The Alzheimer's Association reports the estimated lifetime cost of care for someone with dementia is $357,297.[27]

Of the people who turned sixty-five between 2015 and 2019, 15.2 percent will spend more than $250,000 on long-term care during their lives, according to a 2016 report from the National Association of Insurance Commissioners (NAIC).[28] Fidelity Investments reports that a sixty-five-year-old couple retiring today can expect to spend an average of $295,000 out of pocket on healthcare expenses (not including long-term care, over-the-counter medicines, or most dental care) over the course of their retirement.[29] One way or another, you need to account for these expenses. Ignoring your future healthcare needs can ruin your financial plan.

LONG-TERM CARE POLICIES

Long-Term Care insurance policies aren't cheap. Some insurers have had to hike the premiums they charge their policyholders, while others have just stopped offering long-term care policies. Genworth Financial, for example, recently announced a 58 percent rate hike, while Mass Mutual requested a 77 percent rate hike.[30]

---

[25] LongTermCare.gov. 2020. "How Much Care Will You Need?" https://longtermcare.acl.gov/the-basics/how-much-care-will-you-need.html
[26] Genworth Financial. March 30, 2020. "Cost of Care Survey 2019." https://www.genworth.com/aging-and-you/finances/cost-of-care.html
[27] Alzheimer's Association. 2020. "2020 Alzheimer's Disease Facts and Figures." Pg.49 https://www.alz.org/media/Documents/alzheimers-facts-and-figures.pdf
[28] National Association of Insurance Commissioners & The Center for Insurance Policy and Research. May 2016. "The State of Long-Term Care Insurance: The Market, Challenges and Future Innovations." Pg 43. https://www.naic.org/documents/cipr_current_study_160519_ltc_insurance.pdf
[29] Fidelity Investments. August 3, 2020. "How to Plan for Rising Health Care Costs." https://www.fidelity.com/viewpoints/personal-finance/plan-for-rising-health-care-costs
[30] Greg Iacurci. InvestmentNews. August 9, 2018. "Genworth raises long-term-care

The Long-Term Care Insurance Price Index (LTCIP) for 2018 showed that a sixty-year-old couple who bought a new long-term care insurance policy could expect to pay about $3,490 in their first year for a policy offering a potential benefit of more than $666,000 for coverage they begin needing at age eighty-five[31] Costs can vary widely, though, and so will the precise benefits which are offered in any given policy. Some, for example, will cover just nursing-home care, while others cover both nursing-home care and home healthcare.

Most of these policies will reimburse long-term care expenses from a qualified provider. This means that if you have a permanent cognitive impairment or are unable to perform two out of six activities of daily living, and you hire someone to provide care, your policy may reimburse you for out-of-pocket expenses. The six basic ADLs are eating, bathing, getting dressed, toileting, transferring, and continence.

Besides paying premiums for the rest of your life, the biggest drawback of these types of policies is the fact that if you never needed long-term care, you never received any financial benefit in exchange for all of the paid premiums.

LIFE INSURANCE POLICIES WITH LTC BENEFITS

Because of the aforementioned statistics, life insurance policies with long-term care riders are becoming extremely popular. According to industry-funded research firm LIMRA, 260,000 such policies were issued in 2017 compared to only 66,000 traditional long-term care policies.[32] These policies have three components. One is the tax-free death benefit, second is a cash value feature, and third is a tax-free, long-term care benefit. One of the most attractive features of this type of

---

insurance costs an average 58%." https://www.investmentnews.com/genworth-raises-long-term-care-insurance-costs-an-average-58-75498

[31] American Association for Long-Term Care Insurance. January 2, 2018. "Long-Term Car Insurance Prices Drop AALTCI's 2018 Price Index Reports." https://www.aaltci.org/news/long-term-care-insurance-association-news/long-term-care-insurance-prices-drop-aaltcis-2018-price-index-reports

[32] Ben Mattlin. *Financial Advisor Magazine.* May 1, 2019. "Hybrid LTC Insurance is Popular, But Be Careful." https://www.fa-mag.com/news/hybrid-ltc-insurance-is-popular---but-be-careful-44536.html

policy is that it can be used for supplemental retirement planning as well as long-term care and estate planning.

Unlike traditional long-term care policies, assuming the policy remains in force and sufficiently funded, the policy owner or their beneficiaries will get back at least what was contributed and typically more than what was contributed. These policies can be designed to maximize any of the three components, depending on one's needs. If you are mostly concerned about outliving your money, they can offer access to your policy's cash values via policy loans or withdrawals.[33] However, for those who are looking to maximize the pool of funds available for potential long-term care needs, they should consider purchasing a policy that provides sufficient LTC coverage without focusing heavily on the expectation of account value growth. In either case, these are still life insurance policies. They typically provide significant tax-free death benefits to the beneficiaries if the insured dies without having used the long-term care benefit.

SELF-INSURING

If you have enough assets that you could afford to allocate $250,000 per person for potential long-term care expenses, then you could consider simply paying those expenses on your own. This is a calculation that can be worked into any retirement plan very easily. However, some people don't like the thought of paying so much money out of their pocket at the expense of their heirs, even if they could afford it.

MEDICAID PLANNING

For those who need healthcare or long-term care but lack the resources to pay for it, the United States government will provide this care for free. Medicaid is the federal program that provides healthcare benefits to the

---

[33]Policy loans and withdrawals will reduce available cash values and death benefits and may cause the policy to lapse or affect any guarantees against lapse. Additional premium payments may be required to keep the policy in force. In the event of a lapse, outstanding policy loans in excess of unrecovered cost basis will be subject to ordinary income tax. Tax laws are subject to change. You should consult a tax professional.

indigent. Many people who wind up needing long-term care can pay for it out of their assets, at least initially. However, because the costs can be significant, many people access Medicaid benefits once their assets have been depleted. Medicaid may help with paying for home care, assisted living, and nursing homes.

In an ideal world, many people would like to qualify for Medicaid before they become completely broke, thereby preserving an inheritance for their children. For those who are contemplating transferring all their assets to their children in order to qualify for Medicaid, the government is already one step ahead of you. If you gift any assets to your children, you must wait 60 months from the date you gave the gift before becoming Medicaid eligible. However, there are perfectly legal strategies that one can implement to become eligible for Medicaid while still possessing considerable assets. In fact, there is an entire industry of "elder law" attorneys who specialize in helping people qualify for Medicaid benefits well in advance of their assets becoming depleted.

Assets may be freely transferred between spouses to help gain eligibility for a spouse that needs care. Moreover, many assets are exempt for purposes of gaining eligibility. A primary residence, rental property, certain IRAs, and most cars are all exempt assets. In addition, one can enter into contracts with family members to provide care in exchange for a fee, without a 60-month look-back. With the correct guidance and planning, seniors who require long-term care can receive free government healthcare while preserving assets for their heirs. For those who have a modest amount of assets in addition to their primary residence, it may be smart to seek the counsel of an experienced Medicaid attorney to determine how assets may be repositioned to qualify for Medicaid without being indigent.

CHAPTER SEVENTEEN

Mass Production: Is It Right for Your Portfolio?

The term "mass production" was first used in the 1920s in a New York Times article about Ford Motor Company. The concept of the production of large amounts of standardized items had been used for centuries, but Ford embraced it—relying heavily on assembly line workers to allow for the unprecedented manufacture and delivery of millions of cars throughout America.

These methods allowed the company to reduce costs and substantially increase profits. Many industries have copied and implemented the principles of mass production. Have you ever been in a gated community built by a major home builder? You will likely notice that the houses are all very similar. Typically, the developer will offer the choice of a few different home models because it just isn't cost-effective to build each home from scratch. This results in a simpler, more cost-effective process for all parties. These home developments are often referred to as "cookie-cutter" homes or because they are reminiscent of a batch of cookies that were shaped from a handful of different templates. For those of you who want a custom home, it's usually necessary to find a suitable piece of land, hire an architect, get permits, hire a builder and endure the uncertainty of the actual cost because invariably, there will be unforeseen contingencies and mid-construction additions and changes. But most people are happier with the end product because it was built with their exact needs and specifications in mind.

Many businesses have used principles of mass production to deliver their products and services to the masses. The financial services industry is no exception. The profession has implemented many principles of mass production to deliver investments and financial products to its customers. Large financial services firms need to be able to offer quality control the same way McDonald's needs to make sure that its hamburgers taste the same no matter which store you visit. The hamburgers are unlikely to be the best you are ever going to eat, but they are remarkably consistent, and you almost always get what you are expecting.

In 2020, investment banks such as Merrill Lynch and Morgan Stanley each had over 15,000 representatives.[34] Vanguard has over 16,000 employees and over 30 million customers.[35] It's very difficult to deliver uniform service if each advisor is simply recommending whatever they want to their customers. One of the ways to keep profits up and attempt to create quality control is to create several model portfolios comprised of varying stock/bond percentages designed to be delivered to the masses. Target funds are one example of a common mass-produced investment fund. It's a generic mix of stocks and bonds that automatically decreases exposure to stocks each year as investors get older.

In other instances, customers are instructed to complete a risk profile questionnaire. Based on a customer's risk tolerance, the client is directed to a model portfolio with matching equity exposure. Clients who are more conservative would be placed in a model with a higher percentage of bonds. This approach will typically allow major financial services companies to serve millions of customers with efficiency and profitability. While this mass production of investment services may be profitable for the financial service industry, investors should be comparing the cookie-cutter option to a customized financial plan that is built with their unique needs in mind. While a mass-produced portfolio may not be the worst solution, it's almost certainly not the best one, either.

There are some inherent flaws in the traditional stock/bond portfolio, in my opinion. These models are based on longstanding modern portfolio

---

[34] Owler. 2020. "Merrill Lynch's Competitors, Revenue, Number of Employees, Funding, Acquisitions & News." https://www.owler.com/company/ml

[35] Vanguard. 2020. "Fast Facts About Vanguard." https://about.vanguard.com/who-we-are/fast-facts/.

theory. Bonds tend to do well in times when stocks are going down. This can greatly lower overall portfolio volatility. However, these model portfolios have traditionally enjoyed much higher yields from the bond portion of the portfolio than exist in today's low interest rate environment. In 1980, if you had a 60/40 stock/bond portfolio, a big portion of your portfolio was earning double-digit yields. In 2020, ten-year treasuries yielded less than 1 percent. That's a big difference. Do investors really want a big portion of their portfolios earning less than the inflation rate? How long should we continue to do something simply because that's how it's always been done? Meanwhile, by the end of the last decade, the valuations of stocks have risen to fairly high levels. This is to be expected when interest rates are so low, but stocks have historically had their best decades when stocks had relatively low valuations.

Fortunately, there are other alternatives. Some of the wealthiest investors and institutions aren't investing in target funds or cookie-cutter stock/bond portfolios. They are using many other instruments, including non-public real estate, private equity, private credit, structured notes, and even hedge funds. Many of these strategies, which involve unique risks, have less volatility than stocks and potentially higher expected returns than bonds. In other words, many times it is possible to have potentially higher returns with as much or even less risk.

The wealthiest investors have traditionally had and continue to have access to innovative and exclusive investment opportunities. What about everyone else? These strategies are becoming more and more accessible. The top investment companies like Blackstone, which previously only worked with the wealthiest families and institutions, have rolled out private alternative investments not necessarily for the masses but at least for the mass affluent. You just must know where to look. You're not going to find these alternatives at the Burger Kings of the financial services industry. However, many independent Registered Investment Advisors are starting to include these alternatives in their toolbox. These alternatives are now available to accredited investors in increments ranging from $50,000 to $250,000, as opposed to the historical minimums starting at $5,000,000. One of the attractive features of these investments, as mentioned above, is the relatively low volatility. Unlike a publicly traded investment, which has a share price that fluctuates wildly based on what the public markets are willing to pay for the shares, alternative investments are typically priced monthly or quarterly. The price is based on the value of the underlying assets. For instance, with a publicly traded REIT, it is not uncommon for the share price to trade at a substantial discount to the actual value of the underlying real estate. But when the market tanked in the first quarter of 2020, the Vanguard REIT Index fell about 40 percent from its February level, while finishing the first quarter down almost 30 percent from its high.[36] Meanwhile, one of the largest Blackstone REIT that's been offered to the mass affluent and had been averaging 10 percent annual returns since inception, marked down the value of its shares by less than 8 percent from its prior high.[37] It's a lot easier for most investors to remain calm in the face of an 8 percent loss as opposed to a 40 percent loss. Obviously, past performance is no guarantee of future results, but I believe investors can benefit greatly by increased exposure to the right alternative investments.

---

[36] MarketWatch. 2020. "Vanguard Real Estate ETF." https://www.marketwatch.com/investing/fund/vnq.

[37] Blackstone. BREIT. 2020. "Performance." https://www.breit.com/performance

CHAPTER EIGHTEEN

Structured Notes

As an advisor, one of the things I am always analyzing is risk-adjusted return. In other words, it's not just about how much return is expected from a particular investment, but how much risk are we assuming to hopefully get that expected return. For instance, if my cousin, who never owned a business before, asked me to lend him $100,000 to start a new restaurant, I would consider that riskier than if a successful restaurant owner asked me to lend him $100,000 secured by a mortgage against the building that he owns which will house his new restaurant. Therefore, I would need a much higher expected return from my cousin to even consider his investment. The same analysis goes into every investment we recommend. Many of our clients are not comfortable with a portfolio that is heavily allocated to stocks. They are also looking for steady income in a low interest rate environment. One of the tools we have identified that can be used as an alternative to stocks with less investment risk is structured notes.

A structured note is essentially a bond that is typically issued by one of the large investment banks. The bond—or "note"—is hedged with derivatives designed to create specific financial outcomes predicated on the performance of underlying securities.

These notes are issued with a specific maturity date and, like all corporate bonds, are subject to the credit risk of the issuer. In addition, they are also subject to call risk, lack of liquidity, and the potential for inaccurate pricing.

Most corporate bonds pay periodic stated interest coupons. Structured notes can be designed to pay either fixed interest or can be designed for growth. The performance of these notes can be based on pretty much any marketable security. However, typically the notes are linked to major market indexes like the S&P 500. Based on market conditions, we can design some extremely attractive risk-adjusted expected returns (although, of course, these expected returns are not guaranteed).

Many of the large investment banks, including Goldman Sachs, Morgan Stanley, Barclays, and Citibank, create and issue structured notes. It's important to note that each bank issuing a structured note will have different pricing. Each of the major players in this space, issue "off the shelf" notes that you can buy each month. However, for a $500,000 minimum investment we can go to any bank and ask them to design whatever we want, and we can have each issuer compete to get the best bids. We can then allocate portions of that note across several client accounts.

There are several kinds of notes:

Income Notes: Structured notes can be designed for a relatively high level of income and varying degrees of investment risk. One note we recently issued was a six-year note from Wells Fargo. It pays 10 percent annual interest (2.5 percent quarterly). That interest is paid during each quarter that either the S&P 500, Eurostoxx 50, or Russell 2000 is not down more than 40 percent. In those quarters where the indexes are down over 40 percent since the date of issue, no interest is paid. The note will mature at face value if none of the indexes are down more than 40 percent from their original starting values six years earlier. These income notes can be designed with even greater downside protection in exchange for lower interest payments.

Buffered notes: Buffered notes are designed to provide some downside protection. For example, let's say we have a five-year note against the S&P 500 index. The bond will mature in five years and should be worth the initial investment plus 125 percent of the gains of the S&P 500. That means that if you put in $100,000 and the S&P 500 index is up 50 percent over five years, you would get 1.25 multiplied by 50 percent, or 62.5 percent. Accordingly, your $100,000 would be worth $162,500. However, as we stated, it's also about the risk-adjusted returns. The above-described note also had a 20 percent buffer. That means, if the S&P 500 is down over a five-year period, but down less than 20 percent, the note will still mature at face value and the note holder will incur no losses. If the S&P 500 is down more than 20 percent after five years, there is only a loss to the extent the index is below 20 percent. For example, if five years from the date of your investment, the S&P is 22 percent less than it was five years earlier, you would only lose 2 percent. (22 percent loss/20 percent buffer)

Barrier notes: Barrier notes are like buffer notes in that they allow noteholders to link performance to an index or basket of stocks. Barriers, like buffers, also allow investors to avoid losses if the underlying index is down but has not breached the barrier. However, unlike a buffer, at maturity, if a barrier is breached and has not yet recovered, you lose the full amount of the decrease. The tradeoff, however, is much greater leverage. For instance, we recently created a note that will give the noteholder 165 percent of the lower of the S&P 500 or Dow Jones with a 30 percent barrier. When compared to investing in the funds that comprise the index, this structure arguably provides more upside and less downside.

There are two ways you can acquire structured notes: through a broker who receives a commission from the issuing bank or from a fiduciary advisor who does not receive a commission. In order to pay a commission, the bank must reduce the amount invested into the note to pay that commission. It has been my experience that commission-based structured notes have less attractive terms than notes that do not have commissions taken out. A client recently told me that his friend's broker from one of the large investment banks showed him a note against Apple Tesla and Amazon that pays 15% per year for three years if none of those stocks loses more than 50% of their value. In that scenario, the broker was paid a commission by the issuing bank. However, when I quoted the identical note in the advisory version without any commissions were able to get 26.5% annual interest for the client on the same exact note.

As a fee-only fiduciary advisor, we do not accept any commissions, kickbacks, perks, trips, or benefits whatsoever on any registered investments that we recommend. We design structured notes for our clients with no additional compensation for us as the financial advisor beyond the compensation we already earn through our fees on assets under management. It is actually significant extra work to create and manage the structured note process. However, we are committed to doing what is best for our clients.

Some of the negatives of structured notes include the credit risk of the issuing bank. If the bank becomes insolvent and it isn't bailed out, noteholders become unsecured creditors. They would be ahead of the bank's stockholders but still would likely suffer a loss of principal. If you are worried about a U.S. bank going bankrupt, these notes may not be for you. However, if a major bank were to fail, it's possible the stock market would likely be performing poorly as well. In that case, the stock market would likely be too risky for you too.

Additionally, although most notes with buffers and barriers reduce the impact of a bad market, you still have investment risk. If you need access to the funds, the notes may be sold on the secondary market. While you know exactly what your note will be worth at maturity based on the underlying securities, the secondary market may or may not provide full estimated value in the interim.

Also, certain notes allow the issuer to redeem your note at face value before it matures, in which case you will then have reinvestment risk since we don't know what alternatives will be available at that time.

HOW ARE STRUCTURED NOTES TAXED?

From a tax treatment perspective, you should always consult with a tax professional to verify current tax laws. However, generally speaking:

Principal protected notes and those designed for current income will be taxed as ordinary income. Growth notes without current income are taxed at capital gains rates.

Structured notes can be a good investment under the right circumstances, provided you are well aware of all the risks involved. Some of the potential ways structured notes can benefit you are:

- Creating relatively high levels of income
- Reduction of investment risk
- Increase of expected investment returns
- Diversification

CHAPTER NINETEEN

The Final Chapter

Every book and every life have their final chapters. Unfortunately, in my experience, many people don't spend a lot of time writing the final chapter of their lives. When the chapter is left unwritten, the story will often end in a way that the author never intended. It's important to create a comprehensive estate plan so that one can leave their legacy intact.

One's legacy consists primarily of their reputation and their assets. A person's reputation is defined by how they conducted themselves over their lifetime. Many spend their entire lives amassing a sizeable estate. Depending on one's estate plan one's entire estate may be completely distributed with a few months or it can be administered over many decades. However, you can only make changes to your estate plan until you die. After that, it is set in stone. So, it's imperative to make sure it is set up exactly the way you want it to be.

As an attorney, I spend quite a bit of time helping our clients make sure that their final chapters are written to create their intending legacy. In Florida, as well as most states, each person is born with a default estate plan. At one's death, everything will go to one's spouse, and if there is no spouse, everything will go to one's children, and if no children to one's parents, and if no parents to one's siblings. The process by which these assets are distributed is called probate, which can be expensive and time-consuming. To avoid the probate process and alter the default plan of distribution created by the state, one must create their own estate plan.

Estate planning doesn't necessarily require the use of an expensive attorney. Many assets will pass to one's heirs through the operation of law. For instance, if you own your property jointly with a spouse, those assets will automatically pass to the spouse without probate. Additionally, many assets like retirement accounts, annuities, and life insurance policies have beneficiary designations, which will supersede the distribution enumerated in a will or the default estate plan created by the state. Although investment accounts and bank accounts do not automatically come with beneficiary designations, most institutions allow them to be added in the form of TOD (transfer on death) designations. Essentially all financial assets can be left to one's heirs in exact proportions desired without the need for an attorney. For many people, the only asset which does not come with a beneficiary designation is their home and other real estate.

I once met with a prospective client who stated that they "put their son's name on the deed" to avoid probate. This is not advisable for several reasons. Once you put someone's name on your deed, you can no longer sell or mortgage the property without the permission of that person. The real estate is now subject to the claims of that person's creditors. Finally, if a child inherits your house, they can sell it without paying any taxes on the gains that occurred since you originally purchased it. However, they will not get that tax benefit if you transferred the property to them while you were alive. Luckily, in Florida, there is a simple solution. You can use what is called a Lady Bird deed. This type of deed allows you to add a beneficiary to any piece of real estate. This will allow the property to avoid probate and go directly to the beneficiary. This designation is revocable and can be changed by the property owner at any time.

Although it is possible to create the desired plan of distribution and avoid probate without an attorney, there are many reasons to create a revocable trust. Many people do not want all their assets distributed outright to their heirs. Some heirs might be minors or otherwise unequipped to adequately manage their newfound wealth. Some people are concerned that their assets could wind up going to their child's former spouse in the event of death or divorce. It's also very common to have an heir with a disability that affords them government benefits. A trust with special language must be used to prevent that heir's inheritance from making them ineligible for future government benefits. A trust can be used to allow the grantor to retain some control over how the assets are used and distributed after their death. It's not uncommon for a trust to provide that the assets will be professionally managed, with the income being distributed on a quarterly basis and the principal being accessible under ascertainable standards pursuant to the discretion of a trustee. Often when I review trusts, I notice that the beneficiaries get full control and distribution of assets once they reach a certain age, like 35 or 40. If you want your trust to maintain control over the assets once you are gone, you probably should not have this type of provision in your trust.

One of my elderly clients had a sizeable estate and only one child who was disabled and unable to manage his affairs. The client had a revocable trust, but he did not know who he could name as the trustee to oversee the trust assets and look after his son. My client did not believe that his son would be capable of managing his inheritance or even making basic financial decisions without some assistance. The father had been providing this assistance up until now, but he wouldn't be there forever to do that. This was a very big concern of his because he didn't know who he could rely on to look after his son. Luckily, there are several attorneys I work with who are willing to serve as the trustee in these types of situations for a reasonable fee. In this case, my client named one of these attorneys to serve as trustee before he died.

Following the father's death, the successor trustee seamlessly continued to manage the client's assets for the benefit of his son. He helped the client's son purchase a home. He made sure that the closing was done properly, the right homeowner's insurance was acquired, and even negotiated with a contractor to make the necessary improvements. He set up monthly income and bill pay, so that client's son is taken care of. A few months later, the son called me after his car broke down, not knowing what to do. The trustee helped him get a new, more reliable car. The successor trustee will never replace the father in this situation, but at least the father took comfort knowing that he had a good plan in place.

Even if your kids are financially savvy, leaving them assets in trust, even if the children serve as their own trustees, has certain benefits. The assets will be protected from claims of creditors and divorce. If you leave your children assets directly, those assets could arguably be treated as separate property in a divorce setting *if* the assets aren't commingled with marital property. However, the attempt to keep property separate could create a conflict between your child and their spouse that could have been avoided using a trust. Additionally, the trust can provide, that upon the death of the child, the assets remain in trust for one's grandchildren and not the child's spouse.

Ultimately everyone needs to decide how much control they want to have over their assets and how they want their assets distributed. Once those decisions are made, the correct planning can ensure the desired outcome and preserve one's legacy.

CHAPTER TWENTY

Thinking Big Picture?

For most people, life is a very long time. Whenever you look back on the part that has already gone by, however, time seems to have gone by so very quickly and there are no do-overs. When all is said and done, we all have one shot to create our own ideal life, a rewarding career, the best relationships, a comfortable retirement, and a legacy that we can be proud of. Seldom do we obtain the life that we want by accident. We need to affirmatively create the life we want for ourselves. We should all be doing everything we can to give our lives the most meaning and personal satisfaction. What do we intend to accomplish? How are we planning on contributing to the world? How do we want to be remembered? If you haven't answered these questions yet, your reality may turn out to be different from the one you were hoping for.

But in any case, it's never too late to make the best of the rest of your life. In order to get the life you want, you need to articulate it to yourself. A clear understanding of the desired outcome is the prerequisite to designing and implementing your plan. For many, to create the life they want, they need to make very smart decisions about their money, while utilizing the most effective tools and periodically updating their plan as their circumstances evolve and new goals emerge. Hopefully, this book has provided you with the inspiration to make smart choices and take charge of your finances so that you may obtain the life that you truly deserve.

KEITH SINGER, JD, CFP®

About the Author

Keith Singer was born in Philadelphia, Pennsylvania. He started his first business—selling soft pretzels—at the age of eleven. In 1992, he earned his finance degree from The Pennsylvania State University where he also was a finalist in the AT&T Investment Challenge and started (and sold) a successful house-cleaning business.

As he was growing up, his mother tried to encourage him to become a doctor. While exhibiting very little interest in subjects like biology and chemistry, Singer resisted his mother's influence to study pre-med but instead reached a compromise: He would become a lawyer. By the time Singer was attending law school, he had realized that he loved South Florida and wanted to reside there. He is a cum laude graduate of the University of Miami.

As an attorney, Singer helped clients with probate disputes and realized that as an attorney, he could try to fix people's problems, but if he could help them plan properly, he could help them avoid problems altogether. Therefore, he decided to become a Financial Advisor and Certified Financial Planner™ professional. Since 1996, Singer has been advising clients how to grow, preserve, and distribute their wealth while finding efficient tax solutions. In 2000, he obtained his CLU, a life insurance advanced planning designation from the American College of Financial Services.

For the first ten years of his career, Singer focused on helping younger clients plan for their future retirements. Since then, his practice has shifted to working with those in or near retirement. He continues as an active member of the Florida Bar Association, drafting wills, trusts, and estate-planning documents for his clients. He also advises his clients on a variety of asset protection, income taxation, and estate planning issues.

Keith Singer has been quoted in The Wall Street Journal, U.S. News and World Report, Money Magazine, Business Web, Kiplinger, The New York Times, and NBC, ABC, CBS, and CNBC.

Made in the USA
Columbia, SC
02 June 2025